Aerial and Close-Range
Photogrammetric Technology:
Providing Resource Documentation,
Interpretation, and Preservation

Technical Note 428

BLM

Aerial and Close-Range Photogrammetric Technology: Providing Resource Documentation, Interpretation, and Preservation

By Neffra A. Matthews
Bureau of Land Management
National Operations Center
Denver, Colorado 80225

Technical Note 428
September 2008

ACKNOWLEDGMENTS

I thank my colleagues within the National Operations Center–Division of Resource Services and other offices within BLM who have supported the use of photogrammetry in the Bureau. In addition, I especially thank my coworker, Tom Noble. Several years ago Tom began applying his knowledge of mathematics, surveying, and software programming to photogrammetry. The BLM and the use of close-range photogrammetry in general have greatly benefited from his efforts. I thank the following persons for their reviews of this manuscript:

Alan Bell, USDI, Bureau of Reclamation
Mike Bies, USDI, Bureau of Land Management
Brent Breithaupt, University of Wyoming
Matthew Bobo, USDI, Bureau of Land Management
Debra Dinville, USDI, Bureau of Land Management
Rebecca Doolittle, USDI, Bureau of Land Management
Jason Kenworthy, Oregon State University
Dave Kett, USDI, Bureau of Land Management
Lisa Krosley, USDI, Bureau of Reclamation
Lucia Kuizon, USDI, Bureau of Land Management
Carolyn McClellan, Smithsonian Institution,
        National Museum of the American Indian
Tom Noble, USDI, Bureau of Land Management
Vanessa Stepanak, USDI, Bureau of Land Management
Bill Ypsilantis, USDI, Bureau of Land Management

CONTENTS

Oblique low-level aerial view of Highway 89, Kanab Creek, north of Kanab, Utah.

ABSTRACT

Photogrammetry is the art and science of obtaining precise mathematical measurements and three-dimensional (3D) data from two or more photographs. The Bureau of Land Management has benefited from its in-house photogrammetric capabilities, support, and expertise for more than 20 years. This support includes creating unique and value-added digital datasets and serving as subject matter experts and contracting officer's representatives to obtain aerial photography and other types of 3D data. Traditionally, most people think of photogrammetry in the context of aerial photography. Photogrammetric techniques can be applied to virtually any source of imagery, whether it comes from 35-mm digital cameras or an earth-orbiting satellite. As long as the images are captured with stereoscopic overlap, one can derive accurate 3D data at a very wide range of scales.

The rapid evolution of digital cameras and increasing capabilities of computers and analytical software has dramatically expanded the variety of situations to which photogrammetry may be applied, while simultaneously decreasing the costs of acquisition, processing, and analysis. A variety of resource specialists (such as hydrologists, soil scientists, archaeologists, paleontologists, biologists, range conservationists, and engineers) can greatly benefit from 3D products derived from modern photogrammetric techniques. This is especially true in the field of ground-based or close-range photogrammetry. This document provides a general overview of photogrammetry, with separate sections focusing on traditional aerial photogrammetry and close-range photogrammetry. The appendices contain technical information on the equipment and suggested methods for capturing stereoscopic imagery. Their purpose is to assist field resource specialists in the successful completion of the imagery collection portion of a basic, close-range photogrammetry project.

INTRODUCTION

The United States Department of the Interior, Bureau of Land Management (BLM) is charged with managing almost 104 million ha (256 million acres) of surface land. This vast landscape includes some of the most ecologically and culturally diverse, scientifically important lands in Federal ownership. Documenting and evaluating the present condition—and in some instances, past condition—of its land is a critical part of the Bureau's mission. Not only do these condition data provide information on the health of the land and serve as a basis for future decision making, but they also provide a tool for determining the effectiveness of present management practices. To most efficiently support the BLM's management effort, documentation methods that are quantifiable and repeatable are needed.

A tool for capturing present condition is photography. While visually enlightening, a single photograph is in many ways anecdotal and can be biased by the perceptions of the photographer (Mudge et al. 2006). However, photographs can be taken in such a way as to provide detailed and measurable three-dimensional (3D) data, thus providing a more robust dataset from which an analyst can derive quantifiable information. The science and technology of this process is called photogrammetry (Appendix A). The basic requirement for photogrammetry is an overlapping pair of photographs taken to mimic the perspective centers of human stereoscopic vision. Photography, at virtually any scale (from a pair of images taken from an earth-orbiting satellite to extremely close-up images of a delicate biological soil crust), can be processed by using photogrammetric techniques. The resulting datasets integrate both corrected imagery and 3D surface data that can be viewed, manipulated, and measured by using GIS and other similar software.

Since the 1930s, most of the topographic and thematic maps produced in the United States have been made according to aerial photography and photogrammetric methods. Aerial photography, digital imagery, ground control survey data, and photogrammetry are the basic components for many of the maps and geographic information systems (GIS) data used by the BLM. For more than 20 years, the BLM has maintained some in-house photogrammetric capability with specialized expertise and equipment. This capability assists the Bureau in meeting its unique data needs (e.g., riparian boundary litigation) and by providing large-scale mapping products not available from other government agencies.

Within the last decade, advances in digital imagery and photogrammetric software, combined with lower equipment costs (Matthews et al. 2004), have enabled the use of photogrammetric methods over a wider range of applications, while at the same time reducing equipment costs and decreasing computing times, making the entire process more cost-effective. These advances have revolutionized close-range photogrammetry by removing many of the rigors of traditional aerial photogrammetry, thus moving stereoscopic image collection from the hands of the photogrammetric expert to those of field personnel.

A significant advantage of close-range photogrammetry is that images for a small project can be acquired with minimal field equipment and a small amount of training. Once taken, these images can be processed to a detailed, 3D grid of thousands of precise data points or archived and processed when needed to provide quantifiable measurements of condition. This can support long-term comparisons and provide a visual and metric dataset that cannot be achieved through any other method. Because accurate measurements can be made from the dataset, the resulting determinations are more defensible than simple anecdotal evidence (e.g., a single photo). In addition, these datasets can be more persuasive to both the internal and external audience, thus supporting better-informed conclusions.

In the past year, the 3D measuring and modeling software used to process close-range photographs has increased in its capability and ease of use and decreased in cost. Both traditional aerial and close-range photogrammetric processing are presently limited to BLM staff at the BLM National Operations Center (NOC) and the Alaska State Office. However, software and hardware innovations will continue to increase the accessibility of both stereoscopic processing and viewing, making photogrammetry more accessible within the BLM and providing a cost-effective, responsive, and quantifiable documentation and monitoring technique.

This report is intended to provide resource specialists with an overview of photogrammetry—both traditional aerial and close-range—and to provide examples of projects to which these technologies have been applied. In addition, the appendices contain the requirements of stereoscopic image capture, describe proper camera settings, and outline the basic procedure for field capture of images for a small, close-range project.

WHAT IS PHOTOGRAMMETRY?

Photogrammetry is the science behind the creation of almost every topographic map made since the 1930s. The human ability to perceive depth is the basis for the science (and technology) of photogrammetry. This ability to see in three dimensions is due to the offset in perspective centers between the left and the right eyes. Photographs taken to mimic this perspective shift are referred to as stereoscopic or stereo (meaning two). A stereo pair (or series) of images is taken from consecutive positions and overlap each other by at least 60%. Through the use of photogrammetry, highly detailed three-dimensional data can be derived from the two-dimensional photographs of a stereo pair.

The formal definition of photogrammetry is the art, science, and technology of obtaining reliable information about physical objects and the environment through the process of recording, measuring, and interpreting photographic images and patterns of electromagnetic radiant energy and other phenomena. In many instances, the use of photogrammetry can be more efficient, less labor-intensive, and more cost-effective than other types of field 3D data collection, resulting in products that have a level of detail, accuracy, range, and price that is difficult to match with other technologies (Birch 2006). As described previously, the main component necessary for a photogrammetric project is a series of overlapping stereoscopic images. The stereo images may be captured by a large variety of cameras at almost any height or platform (from tripod to earth-orbiting satellite).

Photogrammetry is informally divided into two basic categories according to the height of the platform—traditional (or aerial) and nontraditional (or close-range). Advances in commercially available and cost-effective photogrammetric software, high-resolution digital cameras, high-performance laptop computers, and unmanned aerial systems (UAS) have caused those categories to overlap in recent years. This document refers to the traditional process of acquiring and using large-format (e.g., 9 × 9 inch; Figure 1), vertical (film or digital) aerial images as aerial photogrammetry. Close range is used to refer to photographs with an object-to-camera distance of less than 300 m.

Figure 1. Example of a large-format (9 × 9-inch) vertical, natural-color, aerial photograph taken at a scale of 1:12,000. The area covered by the image is in north-central Wyoming. The Red Gulch Dinosaur Tracksite lies near the center of the image.

Onboard a Department of the Interior helicopter at Kanab, Utah, Airport preparing to conduct low-level aerial photography of Moccasin Mountain Tracksite.

Aerial photogrammetry utilizes large-format imagery and ground coordinate information to effectively recreate the geometry of a portion of the earth in a virtual environment. In this virtual environment, reliable horizontal and vertical measurements can be made and recorded (or compiled) directly into a geospatial data file. Accurate measurements can be recorded from aerial photographic images, by using traditional methods, only when the following conditions are met: a) stereoscopic image pairs (two or more overlapping photographs) cover the object to be analyzed; b) accurate x, y, and z coordinates are known for at least three defined object points in the overlapping photographs; and c) a calibrated mapping or metric camera is used to take the photographs.

Figure 2. Digital, or softcopy, photogrammetric workstations support stereoscopic viewing and measuring in a 3D environment, where an overlapping pair of images is viewed with special polarized glasses.

The compilation of planimetric features (such as roads and streams) and topographic information (such as digital terrain models [DTM] and topographic contours) from the photographic sources is accomplished through the use of digital stereoscopic instruments. Digital, or softcopy, photogrammetric workstations require specialized software and hardware for viewing a pair of stereo images. In this virtual environment, an experienced operator can link the images with the ground control to collect precise horizontal and vertical coordinates for a point, line, polygon, or surface. The photogrammetric workstation recreates the geometry of the field subject through a series of mathematical operations (Figure 2). These procedures require a high level of expertise and repetition to maintain the operator's skill. The softcopy instrument has analytical capabilities to a submillimeter level. Thus, high-accuracy ground control coordinate positions are needed to fully exploit the analytical capabilities of these instruments (Matthews et al. 2006).

Aerial Photogrammetry Workflow

Most large-format aerial photography is acquired through commercial contractors and is available in hard copy (film) or digital formats. With the exception of the BLM Alaska State Office, the Bureau does not have the capability to acquire large-format aerial imagery without the assistance of a commercial contractor. In most instances, it is best to work through photogrammetric specialists, such as the staff of the Division of Resource Services (DRS) at the NOC to ensure that the technical and user requirements are met. It is important to begin planning for the acquisition of imagery early in the project. Many elements need to be considered to ensure that project requirements are met (e.g., size of the area, terrain, vegetation cover, sun angle, type of sensor, and product accuracy).

Generally, aerial acquisition is designed and planned according to the specifications needed to generate a particular product with a specific scale and accuracy. The desired resolution dictates the height at which the contractor must fly to acquire the imagery. The following equation states the relation between scale and flying height of the aircraft (Hussain and Bethel 2004).

$$scale = \frac{focal\ length}{flying\ height\ above\ terrain}$$

For example; when film-based aerial photography is flown at a height of 305 m (1,000 feet) above mean terrain with a 153-mm (6-inch) focal length lens, the resulting photography has a scale of 1:2,000. With the resolving power of modern natural color film, the smallest object that can be detected is 5 cm. The distance of the sensor from the subject in commercial aerial photography is restricted by the altitude at which the plane can operate safely. In addition, the Federal Aviation Administration (FAA) imposes a minimum altitude limit of 1,000 feet above populated areas.

Many land management agencies, including the BLM, maintain collections of historical aerial photography of the lands they manage. The National Agriculture Imagery Program (NAIP) is managed by the U.S. Department of Agriculture Farm Services Agency (FSA) and acquires imagery of agricultural lands in the United States. Other governmental agencies work with the FSA to produce statewide coverage of natural-color, 1-, 2-, and 10-m resolution imagery that has been corrected for terrain and image distortions and is geospatially correct (orthorectified) on a cyclical basis. Information on these archives is available through individual agency websites. The BLM's aerial photography archive is maintained at the NOC.

Traditional, large-format (9-inch × 9-inch) aerial photography is film-based and is available in black and white, natural color, or color infrared formats depending on the project requirements. Each aerial camera has its own camera calibration report. This is a report generated with the results of a series of tests developed to reveal the geometric characteristics of the camera and lens. The photogrammetrist uses this information in subsequent calculations to remove distortions, which helps to ensure a high-quality product. However, the imaging and mapping industry has started to migrate to a fully digital process in recent years. Often, traditional film is not used, as the imagery is captured in a digital format.

Presently, several sensor systems are able to capture aerial images digitally. The frame digital sensor is similar to a film camera in that it captures single frames. A push broom sensor (an array of several thousand charge coupled device [CCD] sensors) continuously collects data and then divides the data into frames. Digital images can also be captured in panchromatic, multispectral, and infrared modes simultaneously. This is advantageous because the images may be captured concurrently and do not require additional flights. Digital sensors also offer capabilities that allow the photogrammetrist to enhance portions of the image through image processing techniques to compensate for adverse conditions such as shadows or high-contrast areas. This allows data collection in areas that might be obscured on film.

Project Implementation

Many elements need to be considered to ensure that proper project design is met. These elements include the size of the area, scale of the photography, terrain (mountains or rolling hills), vegetation cover (desert or forest), accessibility (rivers, cliffs, or ownership restrictions), sun angle (latitude, longitude, or time of year), and type of sensor. Perhaps the most important consideration is determining the level of accuracy necessary for the final product. Accuracy, photographic scale, and project size are directly related. Typically, the higher the level of accuracy required, the larger the scale of photography necessary, which in turn affects the magnitude and complexity of the job.

Photo Layout and Flight Line Index Map

One of the most important goals of project design is to ensure that there will be complete stereoscopic coverage of the area of interest, at the proper scale. Photo layout is a depiction of the extent of each photo in relation to the desired area of coverage. The graphic representation of the photo layout is often referred to as a flight line index map. Depending on the final photo scale, the flight line index map for traditional aerial photography flights are designed on 1:100,000- or 1:24,000-scale topographic or digital orthophoto maps (Figure 3). When designing the flight line, care must be taken to ensure that there is complete overlap between photographs. If more than one line of photographs is needed, there must be adequate side lap between the photos.

Survey Control

Another vitally important part of this process is the ground control survey. The survey is the link between the ground and the aerial photography. Surveys give the geospatial products their identity with regard to projection, coordinates, and final accuracy. A high level of accuracy (geodetic quality) is of the utmost importance when gathering the survey (horizontal and vertical) data. Locations for ground survey control points are indicated in the flight line map. Correct spacing and location of ground control survey points determine the area that can be mapped. Before the aerial photography acquisition, ground control panels or targets must be placed on the ground as indicated by the flight line index map (Figure 4). A center point for each panel will be indicated by a monument (often with a survey nail or rebar driven into the ground). To make this point meaningful on the final aerial photographs, large "legs" of white material will be nailed down in a cross centered on the nail or

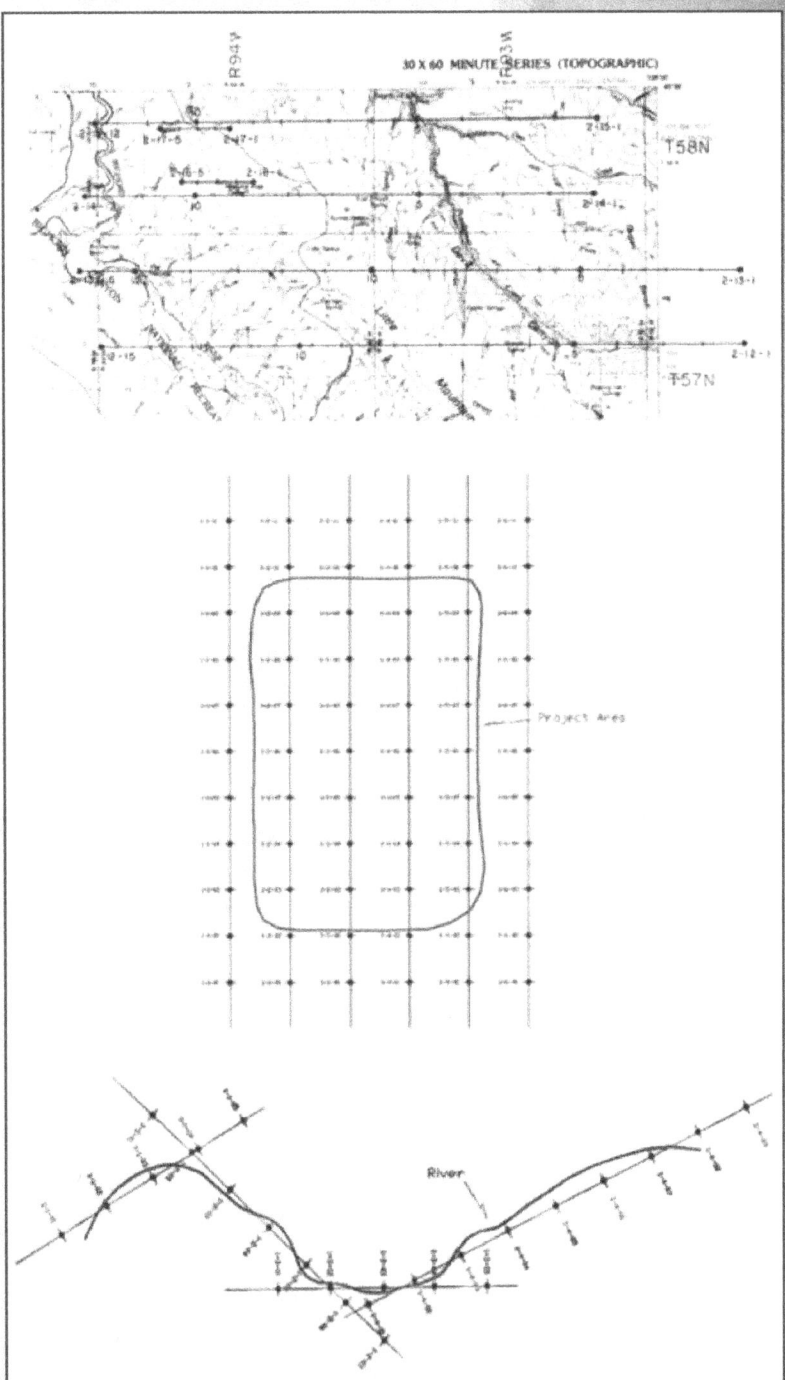

Figure 3. Examples of flight line maps and photo layouts.

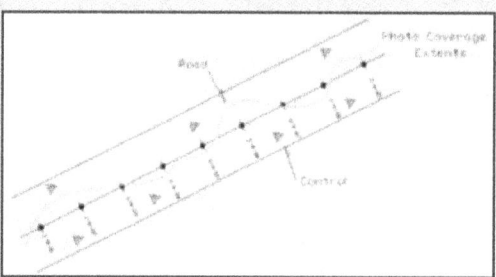

Figure 4. Example of a simple, flight line layout indicating ideal locations for survey control points.

rebar. Ideally, high accuracy horizontal and vertical coordinates for each paneled point will be surveyed before the aerial photography acquisition.

Image Acquisition

After the project requirements have been developed and the flight line and control layouts have been designed, a specification package goes out to bid. At this time standard contracting procedures and schedules come into play. After the contract is awarded, coordination must take place between the contractor, NOC DRS staff, and the field office to ensure the ground control targets are in place before imagery is acquired. After the imagery is acquired, a review copy is provided to the Contracting Officer's Technical Representative for inspection. Once it has been determined that the aerial photography meets the contract specifications, the imagery is accepted. The aerial film and paper prints (if requested) or digital files are then provided to the NOC for processing and inclusion in the BLM's aerial photography collection.

Interpreting the Imagery

The process of extracting data from the aerial imagery begins with combining the digital imagery with the ground control coordinate data. These imagery files can be supplied directly from a digital sensor or by scanning aerial film. Film scanning is performed with an extremely accurate

(micrometer accuracy level) scanner. The result is a digital representation of the film. The photogrammetric workstation re-creates the geometry of the field subject through a series of mathematical calculations. Aerotriangulation is a mathematical process (least squares bundle adjustment) by which the survey data are used to tie the photos together and adjusted coordinate values are distributed throughout the entire project. The oriented image files are displayed on a computer monitor in a way that enables the operator, equipped with a pair of specially designed glasses, to view the digital image files in a 3D environment. In this virtual environment the photogrammetrist can record (or compile) the horizontal and vertical data necessary for producing a reliable map directly into a geospatial data file.

Photogrammetrically Derived Products

A large variety of 3D digital data in support of land use planning and decision making can be developed from both aerial and close-range photography. The photogrammetric process enables the interpretation of imagery and the collection of data necessary to produce reliable maps that support land managers' decisions and are defensible in court. These data customarily take the form of topography (terrain or land surface) or planimetric (such as streams, transportation routes, vegetation boundaries, and cultural) information.

Digital Terrain Model

A digital terrain model (DTM) provides a digital representation of the terrain surface. A DTM can be produced in a manual or automated mode. Manual mode is a process in which a specialist, using a photogrammetric workstation, observes each point in accordance with a specified spacing and records its location, both horizontally and vertically. Automated digital terrain extraction is commonly referred to as autocorrelation or digital image matching. It is a process in which sophisticated software matches pixels (picture elements) with unique spectral and geospatial values in one digital image to similarly valued pixels in the adjacent image of the stereo pair. The addition of more information, such as breaklines (polylines in which each vertex has its own x, y, z, location) may be required to aid the software in determining pixel matches in difficult-to-interpret areas. Topographic contour lines can be generated by using DTM, breakline, and planimetric data.

Digital Orthophoto

A digital orthophoto is a photograph that has been corrected to eliminate distortions and differences in scale (Figure 5a.). The effects of camera tilt and relief displacement (features at higher elevations are displaced away from the center of the photo) are the main causes of these distortions. To eliminate these, the ground geometry is re-created as it would appear from directly above each point in the photo. This is accomplished by applying a process called differential rectification to each pixel in the image. The resulting corrected image can be used as a map.

The orthophoto can be printed as a standalone product or displayed as a backdrop with other spatial information. Perspective views can be produced by draping the orthophoto image over the terrain surface. This process allows one to make a "virtual" visit to the area. The parameters of this virtual surface can be further manipulated to enhance, exaggerate, or isolate a certain feature or part of the image. Topographic contours and planimetric data can be draped onto the orthophoto in three-dimensional space. This virtual visit can be extremely useful for land use planning decisions and communicating with the public.

Vector Map

Vector data customarily take the form of topography (terrain or land surface) or planimetric (streams, transportation routes, vegetation, and cultural) information. Planimetric features are compiled in a manual mode, in which the photogrammetric operator digitizes (in real-world coordinates) points, lines, or polygons representing features of interest (Figure 5b and 5c). The resulting data files can be imported directly into ArcMap for GIS use or into AutoCAD for engineering design.

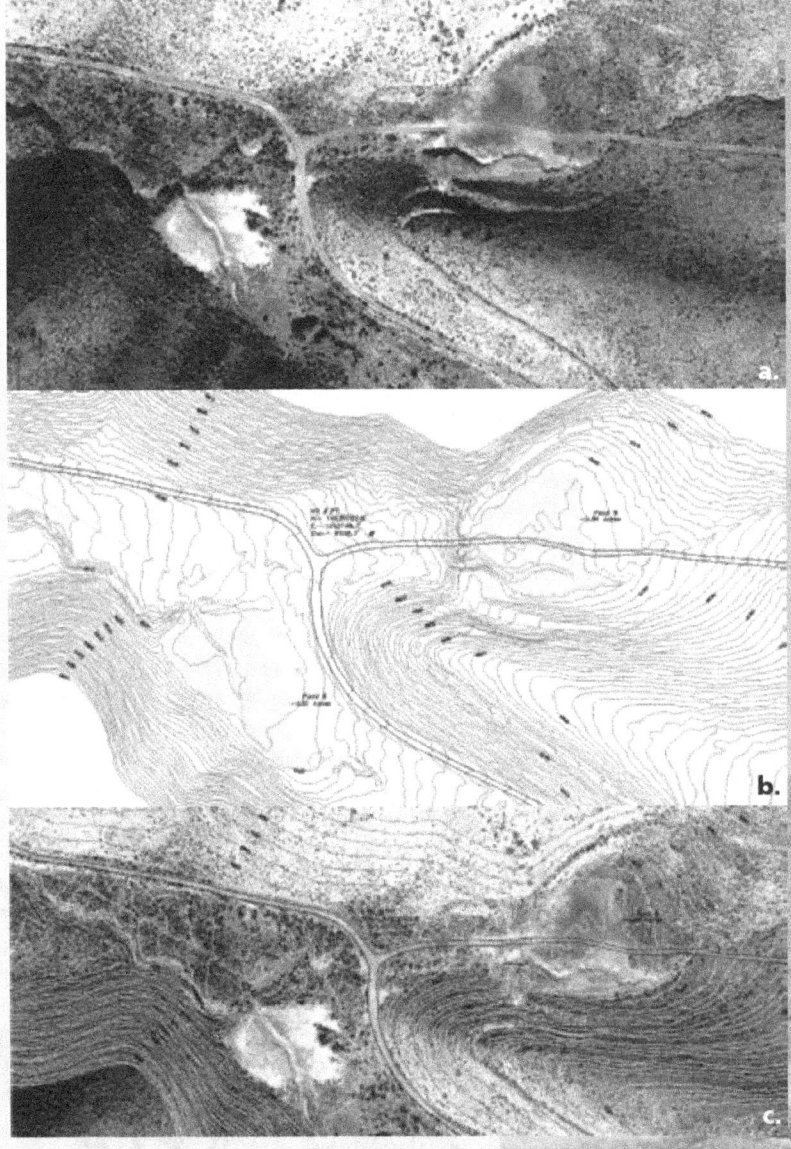

Figure 5. a. Digital orthophoto map. b. Vector map depicting roads and topography. c. A combination of the vector map overlain on the digital orthophoto map. These digital products were created photogrammetrically at the BLM National Operations Center (Denver, Colorado) in support of remediation at the Rip Van Winkle Mine site in Elko County, Nevada.

Imagery captured from a variety of perspectives such as this image of a mesa west of Kanab, Utah, can be acquired from aerial platforms.

CLOSE-RANGE PHOTOGRAMMETRY

The same basic principles of traditional aerial photogrammetry can be applied to stereoscopic pictures taken from lower altitudes or from the ground. Terrestrial, ground-based, and close-range are all descriptive terms that refer to photos taken with an object-to-camera distance of less than 300 m (1,000 feet). This distance equates to the minimum safe flying height above populated areas, as required by the FAA. Since the same basic principles apply to photographs taken from a camera mounted on a tripod (terrestrial) or suspended from a light sport aircraft (low-level aerial), both types of nontraditional photogrammetry are referred to in this report as close-range photogrammetry (CRP).

A variety of cameras and platforms may be used to obtain the photographic images to be used in CRP processing, including cameras housed in unoccupied airborne vehicles, suspended below helium-filled blimps, and mounted on tripods (Figure 6; Breithaupt et al. 2004). Through the use of these nontraditional methods, a resolution or ground sample distance of 0.25 mm and a spatial accuracy equivalent to 0.025 mm can be achieved. Theoretically, there is no limit to the resolution that can be achieved from CRP images (Matthews et al. 2006).

The BLM's national center in Denver has used close-range photogrammetric techniques to document resources since the late 1980s. At that time, although producing high-quality results, the close-range photogrammetric process could be tedious and time-consuming mainly because of the need to apply traditional techniques, workflow, and equipment to close-range image capture and processing. However, recent advances in commercially available and cost-effective three-dimensional measuring and modeling (3DMM) software, high-resolution digital cameras, and high-performance laptop computers have revolutionized the CRP process. With these advances, the photogrammetric process can be moved from the laboratory environment into the field, and taken strictly from the hands of the photogrammetry expert and moved to the hands of the resource specialist.

Figure 6. A variety of cameras and platforms may be used to obtain the photographic images used in close-range photogrammetric processing, including cameras housed in unoccupied airborne vehicles, suspended below helium-filled blimps, and mounted on tripods. All images were taken at the BLM's Red Gulch Dinosaur Tracksite in Wyoming.

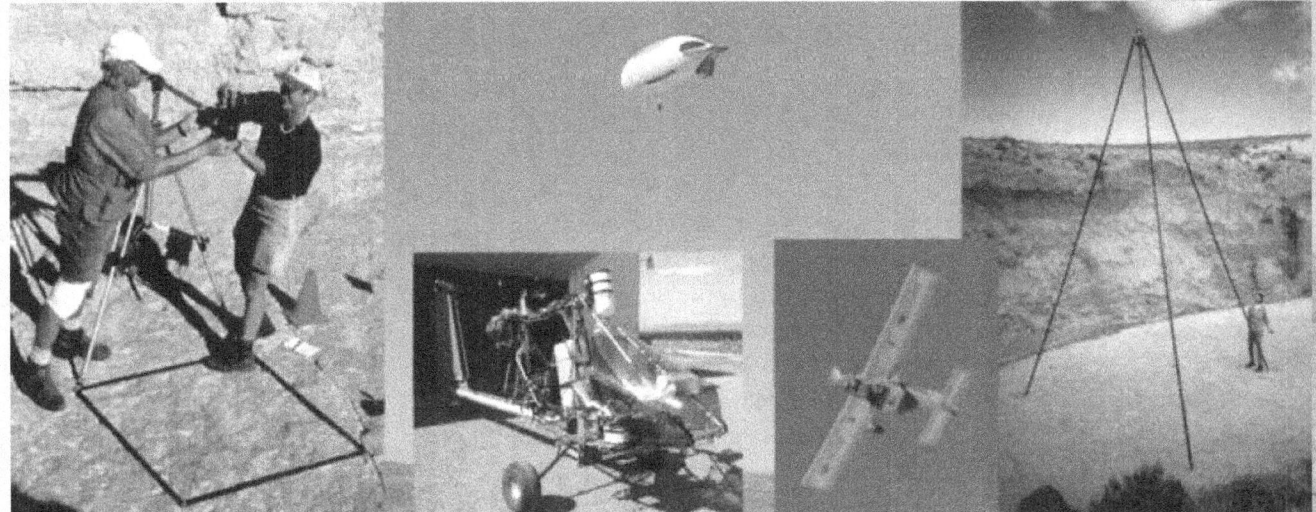

Close-Range Photogrammetry Workflow

As with traditional photogrammetry, the first step in the close-range project workflow is establishing project requirements. These requirements include the area to be covered, type of ground cover, access to areas surrounding the subject, weather, accuracy of the final product, format of the final product, public visitation at the site, and others. However, with the relatively recent availability of reasonably priced, high-quality digital cameras and 3DMM software, many of the traditional requirements in the photogrammetric process can be accomplished in nontraditional ways, providing a high level of flexibility.

An example of the increased flexibility can be seen in image acquisition. In most situations, a person who is experienced with CRP (such as the staff at the NOC), using a high-resolution commercial digital single-lens reflex (SLR) camera, can successfully capture ground-based photographs for a variety of projects. Most persons, following a few simple rules and taking good-quality photographs, can capture the images necessary for completing a successful CRP project. See Appendix C for more details on taking proper photographs and camera requirements and settings.

Project Design

Once project requirements have been determined, the process of project planning can begin. Accuracy, photographic scale, and project size are directly related. Typically, the higher the level of accuracy required, the larger the scale of photography necessary, which in turn increases the magnitude of the job. CRP projects can be placed into one of two categories. These categories are small (simple) and large (complex).

Small projects are those for which the area of interest is equivalent to about 5 m² or smaller. This type of project may also be referred to as extreme close range, as a high precision of data points is expected. Although proper planning strengthens any project, the small terrestrial project may afford greater flexibility in the planning process. Project design and image acquisition for projects of this scope may be successfully carried out by the resource specialists in the field. By following a set of standard operating procedures (Appendix C), successful completion of the capture of imagery for an extreme close-range project may be accomplished.

Large projects are those for which the area of interest is greater than 5 m² or where complexities of terrain or access add to the level of expertise needed for planning and execution of the project. Projects that fall into this category may require a preliminary site visit or the inspection of overview photographs taken of the area. A preliminary reconnaissance of the area will determine if close-range photogrammetry is the best method for data capture, and if so, estimate resources necessary to accomplish the project. Also at this time, the data requirements and expectations of the end user can be discussed. Projects of this scope are best accomplished by those who have experience with close-range image capture and processing.

Sometimes the needed vantage points to capture imagery may not be present, necessitating alternatives to ground-based capture. In these situations, a large ladder, aerial blimp, UAS, or other type of elevated platform may be needed. For these reasons, it is advantageous to contact the photogrammetric specialist for consultation early in project development to help with such items as budget, scheduling, site visit input, and others.

Photo Layout

Close-range photogrammetric projects have more latitude in their design and execution than do traditional aerial projects because the 3DMM software is more capable of handling photographs taken at oblique angles to the subject and in connecting lines of stereophotos that have less consistent overlap than conventional aerial photogrammetry software. Nonetheless, knowing the lay of the land in advance can be critical to project success. This type of evaluation can be gained either through an onsite visit (which is preferable for complex projects) or from inspection of existing imagery. This imagery may take the form of snapshots of the area taken from the ground or existing, small-scale aerial imagery. It is a good investment in time and resources to investigate the existence of digital orthoimagery, which may be available over the Internet, or historical, large-format aerial photography available from agency collections. Site reconnaissance not only aids in identifying strategies for capturing complete stereoscopic coverage of the subject, but can also be used to identify obstacles to imagery acquisition. These obstacles most often take the form of vegetation, which can obscure points of view and terrain issues. Terrain obstacles can range from a lack of an elevated perspective to perilous drop-offs adjacent to the subject of interest.

While the formal flight line index map described previously in the aerial photogrammetry section may be bypassed for simple close-range projects, preplanning can certainly maximize field time, as it would calculate the object-to-camera distances, proper base-to-height ratio, and size and number of reference targets. However, flight line planning is advised for complex projects, especially those using photographs taken from a light sport aircraft or UAS. In these instances, a formal flight line index map may be required to convey expectations to the pilot.

Survey Control

"Surveyed" ground control is not needed for a CRP. During the 3DMM processing, the camera lens system is calibrated. This technique elevates the camera from simply a device for capturing images to a virtual surveying and data collection instrument. By placing an object of known length in the overlap area of stereo models, a very accurate coordinate system can be created. However, GPS survey does give the products an identity as far as projection, coordinates, and final accuracy are concerned and can be easily integrated into a CRP project.

Image Acquisition

The increased flexibility provided by CRP is most completely realized in the image acquisition. Because many of the rigors imposed by traditional photogrammetric processing are removed from CRP, almost any person who can take good quality photographs can take the photos necessary for 3D data processing (see Appendix A). This can be most successfully realized when field personnel have undergone training or thoroughly read this technical note and have completed their own small project. For a large CRP project, a person who is experienced with CRP, such as the staff at the NOC, can successfully capture ground-based photographs for a variety of projects.

When the needed vantage points to capture stereoscopic imagery cannot be attained from a ground-based setup, it will be necessary to investigate more "airborne" options. This may include simply using a ladder or elevated platform to obtain the needed perspective. However, when the area to be documented is large and there is no opportunity for oblique image collection, it may be necessary to employ the use of some type of low-level aerial system. In such instances, it will probably be necessary to go through a commercial provider as is done with traditional aerial imagery acquisition.

Interpreting the Imagery

The process of extracting data from the CRP imagery is another area where increased flexibility is realized compared to traditional aerial photogrammetry. The 3DMM software can run very efficiently on most laptop computers. Thus, processing of digital images may begin in the field as soon as the imagery is acquired and downloaded. This can provide a real time look at the success of the photography coverage and provide for near real time measuring and recording of features. In addition, the photographs may be taken by trained field personnel and archived for later processing in a workstation environment. The resulting 3D image files can be, in turn, sent back out to field personnel for viewing in free viewer software. If more in-depth analysis is required, ArcGIS Stereo Analyst and LIECA Photogrammetric Suite (LPS) (both available within the Bureau) can be used for data compilation.

Figure 7. a. Digital orthophoto map. b. Vector map depicting topography. c. Digital terrain surface colorized by elevation. These maps were produced by photogrammetry at the BLM National Operations Center (Denver, Colorado) with a tripod-based camera and close-range photogrammetric techniques; they depict a dinosaur trackway from the BLM's Red Gulch Dinosaur Tracksite in Wyoming.

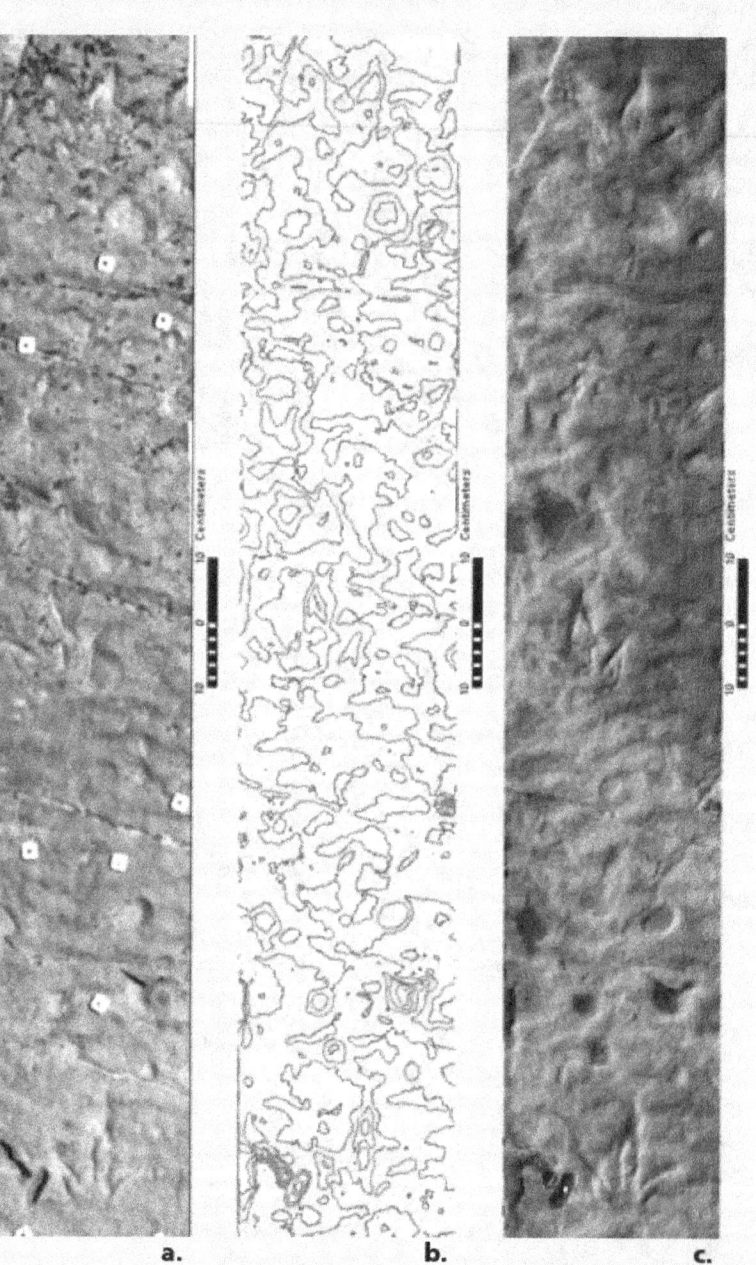

a.   b.   c.

Close-Range Photogrammetry Products

The same cadre of products (digital terrain model, digital orthoimagery, vector maps, and others) that can be created from traditional aerial photogrammetry can also be generated from CRP (Figure 7). In addition, new and unique visuals can be easily produced from within the 3DMM software (Figure 8). Therefore, it is much more efficient to produce animations and digital-rotatable 3D objects that can be integrated into 3D raster streaming Web technology. A 3D Adobe Portable Document Format (PDF) file can be produced and embedded in PowerPoint presentations and documents. In addition, the dense and accurate 3D surface files can be used to produce solid model printouts using a variety of techniques at very large scales, even 1:1.

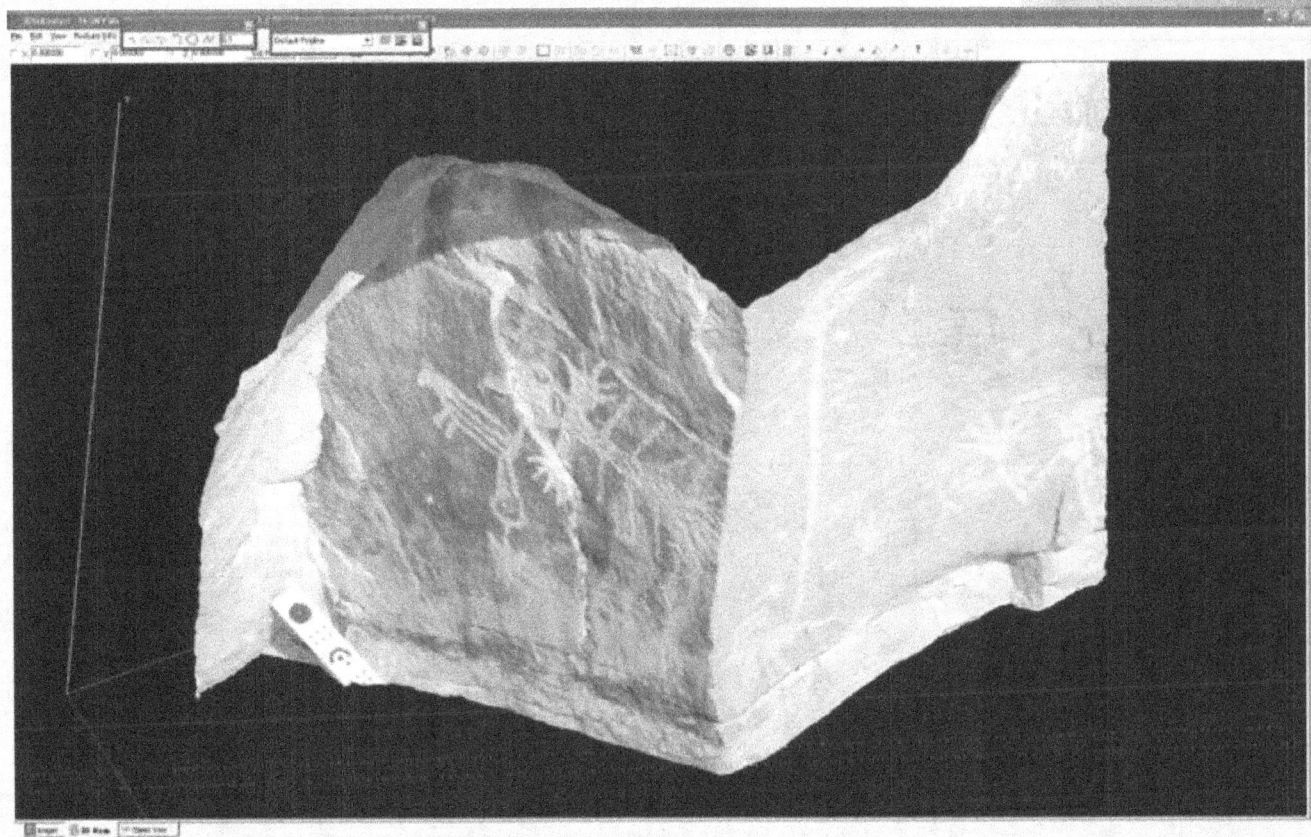

Figure 8. Three-dimensional surface and image datasets can be packaged as industry standard files that can be viewed and rotated in 3D by a number of software programs. Shown is a right angle cliff face from the Bighorn Basin, Wyoming.

Getting a better vantage point to photograph a test plot in the Falcon Road Open OHV area within the Gunnison Gorge National Conservation Area near Montrose, Colorado.

Cyclic Documentation for Change Detection

The ability to detect small changes in soil movement can provide valuable insight for assessing the effects of surface disturbing activities across the landscape (Matthews et al. 2007). Close-range photogrammetry is an excellent method for capturing detailed information about changes, such as erosion, on scales ranging from 1 square meter plots up to an entire hillslope. CRP is especially effective for monitoring erosion on areas that are devoid of vegetation, such as roads, OHV trails, and construction sites (Ypsilantis, personal communication).

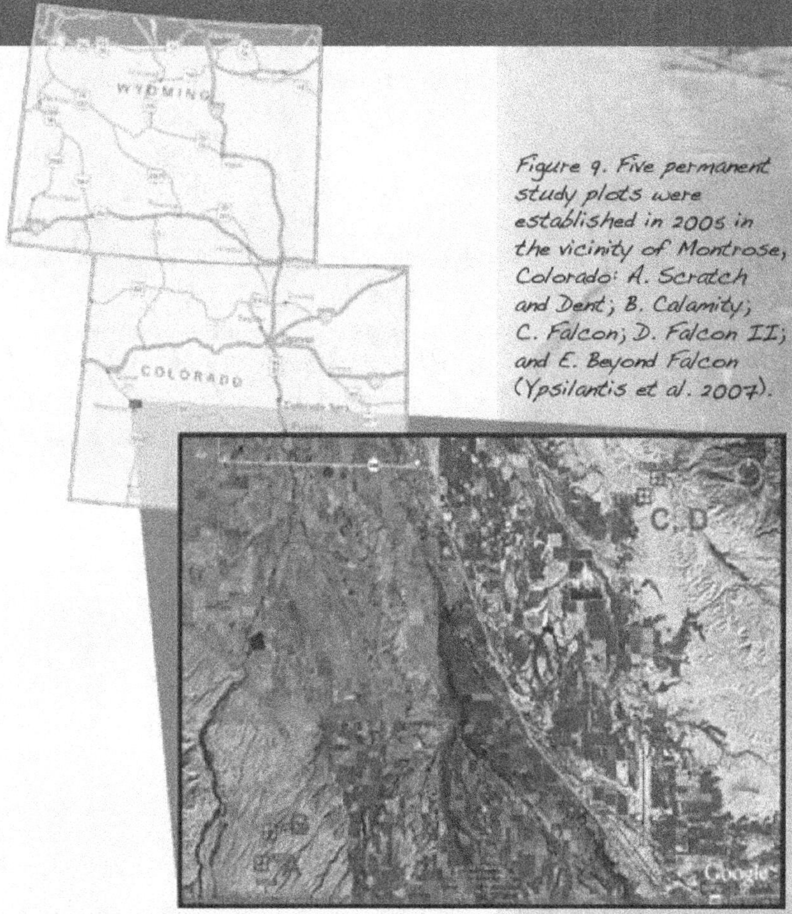

Close-range photogrammetry was used to create 3D surface information to help quantify effects from rapidly increasing off-highway vehicle (OHV) use in the BLM's Uncompahgre Field Office. In August 2005, five permanent, variable-sized plots were established north of Montrose, Colorado. Two sites are located in dry wash channels, which cut through sandstone, shale, and coal, in the Dry Creek Extreme OHV Area. An additional three sites were located in the Falcon Road open OHV area within the Gunnison Gorge National Conservation Area (Figure 9) on adobe badlands composed of Mancos shale (Ypsilantis et al. 2007).

Natural features, such as bedrock (when present outside the traveled area) or rebar plot control stakes, served as *x, y, z* coordinate reference points. The rebar plot stakes were buried beneath the soil surface to ensure that the permanent reference points were not disturbed and to eliminate safety hazards for recreational users. A series of stereoscopic photographs were taken of the plots, concurrently with the camera calibration photographs, to facilitate stereoscopic viewing and analysis of the subject area. Establishing plots, site

Figure 9. Five permanent study plots were established in 2005 in the vicinity of Montrose, Colorado: A. Scratch and Dent; B. Calamity; C. Falcon; D. Falcon II; and E. Beyond Falcon (Ypsilantis et al. 2007).

preparation, and photographing for all five plots were accomplished in 2 days.

In September 2006, the five plots were reestablished and site preparation, GPS coordinate collection, and photography were conducted in 1 day. Real-time kinematics (RTK) GPS positions (accurate to <1 cm) were taken for the control monuments and selected points within each plot locality. The resulting coordinate data were used to tie the digital terrain models to a real-world coordinate system (NAD83 Colorado Central State Plane Zone). In addition, this control was used to process both the 2005 and 2006 photography to aid in ensuring positional integrity between the 2 years (Ypsilantis et al. 2007).

Ten unique, highly detailed 3D surface datasets were produced photogrammetrically. The estimated vertical accuracy of these data is between 0.1 and 1.0 cm. The ten (2 years for each of five plots) 3D digital terrain datasets were analyzed in ArcGIS by using ArcMap and ArcScene. This process included creating a tin surface from the 3D datasets, converting the tin to a grid, and generating a hillshade from the grid (Figure 10). The grids were created with a resolution of 3 cm. Cut-and-fill and surface subtractions were made using the surface grids (Figures 10 and 11). According to the results of the analysis of the surfaces, all five sample plots exhibit loss and gain (or movement) of soil.

The soil gains and losses on the Mancos Shale hillslopes in the Gunnison Gorge NCA are high, with average soil loss rate of 163, 219, and 121 tons/acre calculated for the three sites. Figure 11b illustrates an area of high impact at the top of the slope at one site and an area of minimum impact at a similar slope position. The soil loss for the area of high impact was 585 tons/acre and 367 tons/acre for the area of minimum impact. This indicates that soil loss is greater in the dirt bike trail entrenched into the hillslope than in the area that showed little visual evidence of recent OHV use (Ypsilantis et al. 2007).

Figure 10. Falcon II plot. a. Photograph taken in August 2005. b. 3D surface model generated from the 2005 photography rendered as a hillshade. c. Photograph taken in September 2006. d. 3D surface model generated from the 2006 photography rendered as a hillshade (Ypsilantis et al. 2007).

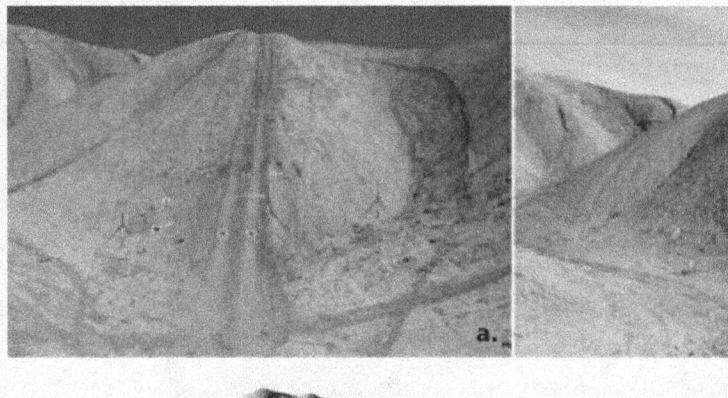

Figure 11. Falcon II plot. The 3D surfaces generated from the 2005 and 2006 photography were compared in ArcGIS. a. Graphic generated by using surface subtraction of the 2005 surface from the 2006 surface. The dark blue and dark red colors represent areas of greatest separation between the two surfaces. b. Falcon II plot. Volumetric loss between 2005 and 2006 for two areas of 17.77 m² (Ypsilantis et al. 2007).

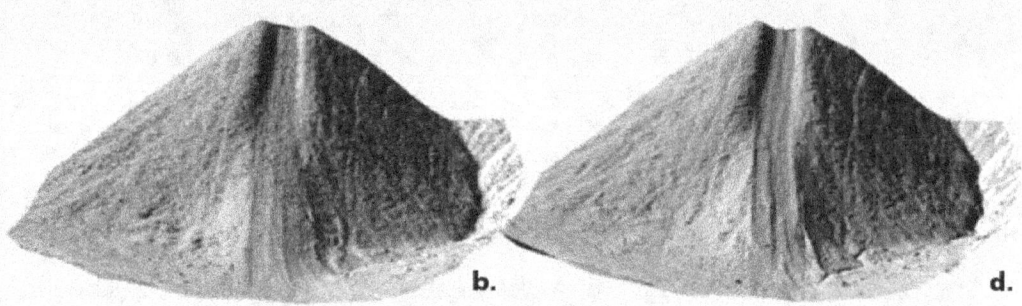

Area of high impact experienced a loss of 1.77 cubic meters.

Area of minimum impact experienced a loss of 1.11 cubic meters.

The Dry Creek Basin sites were along a trail in an ephemeral drainage area. The modified OHVs on the trail can climb boulders and dig the sides of their tires into the hillslopes (Figure 12). This results in deposition of soil material below that hillslope, which is available for transport by the stream during high precipitation. One interesting anomaly shown in Figure 13 is the two large boulders that have been moved approximately 2 m downslope, apparently by OHV activity. The amount and direction of movement could be reliably determined through the use of stereoscopic images taken during the study.

The results of the study were compiled into a report (Ypsilantis et al. 2007) and provided to the Uncompahgre Field Office for use in the travel management plan. In addition, graphics generated from the report are being used in public presentations in support of management decisions.

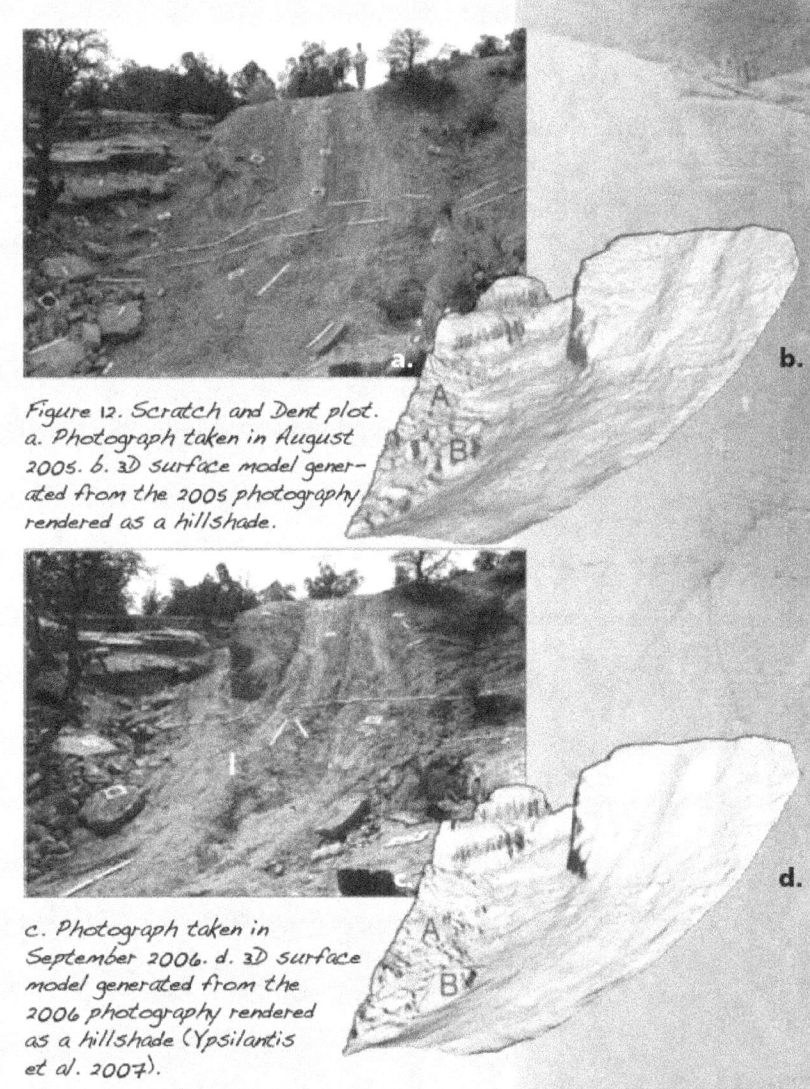

Figure 12. Scratch and Dent plot. a. Photograph taken in August 2005. b. 3D surface model generated from the 2005 photography, rendered as a hillshade.

c. Photograph taken in September 2006. d. 3D surface model generated from the 2006 photography rendered as a hillshade (Ypsilantis et al. 2007).

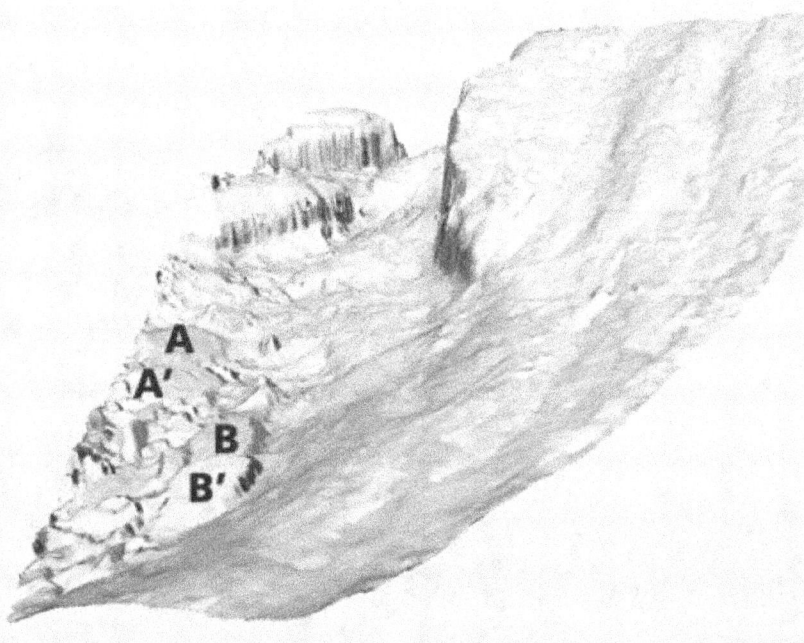

Figure 13. Scratch and Dent plot. Two boulders (A and B), each approx 1 × 0.6 × 0.5 m, moved about 2 m down the channel (A' and B') between August 2005 and September 2006 (Ypsilantis et al. 2007).

Integrating Multiscale Imagery for Riparian Habitat

Coalbed methane discharge water has the potential to influence aquatic and riparian habitats in and along the Powder River of northeastern Wyoming (Figure 14). The Powder River Aquatic Task Group is investigating the use of remote sensing data and techniques to develop economical and effective means of monitoring change in affected aquatic and riparian habitat (Figure 15). This study is evaluating the utility of very large scale aerial (VLSA) imagery for classifying riparian and aquatic habitat types, as well as testing close-range photogrammetric, stereo-based image modeling techniques for change detection, documentation of vegetation composition and structure, and quantifying bank erosion and stability (Bobo et al., 2008).

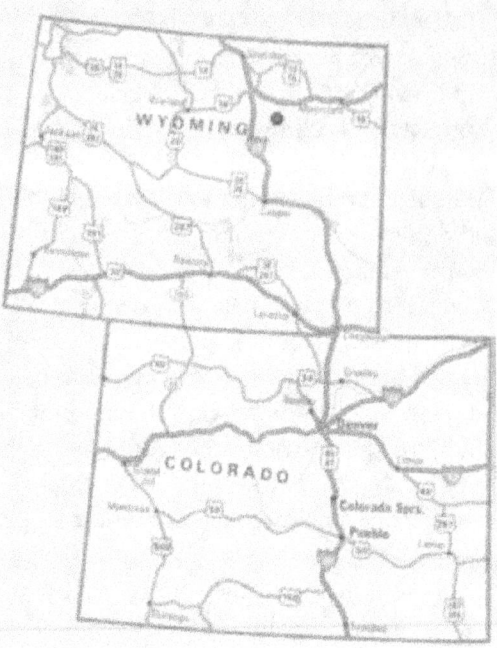

Figure 14. Location map for the Powder River, Wyoming, coalbed methane aquatic monitoring study (Bobo et al. 2008).

A transect-based aerial-sampling protocol was proposed for the first phase of this project to facilitate the capture of ground control to support the CRP work. In related work, the integration of GPS/IMU systems with CRP techniques to accurately and rapidly geocorrect VLSA photography is being explored. The georeferenced VLSA imagery can in turn be used as training data for wider area mapping by using satellite platforms such as Quickbird. Georeferencing of the VLSA imagery is presently conducted with both 0.60-m resolution Quickbird imagery and 0.25-m resolution AeroCam imagery (Noble et al. 2008; Figure 16). Once the spatial links between the three sets of imagery were set, the VLSA was used as a classification tool for the more coarse resolution imagery.

Figure 15. 3D image model developed from close-range photogrammetry along the Powder River, Wyoming. Images from two different times of year are merged to highlight the change in vegetation. With the 3D information available from multi-temporal 3D dataset, changes in vegetation heights, bank erosion, slope, water depth, vegetative cover, and bare ground can be measured (Noble et al. 2008).

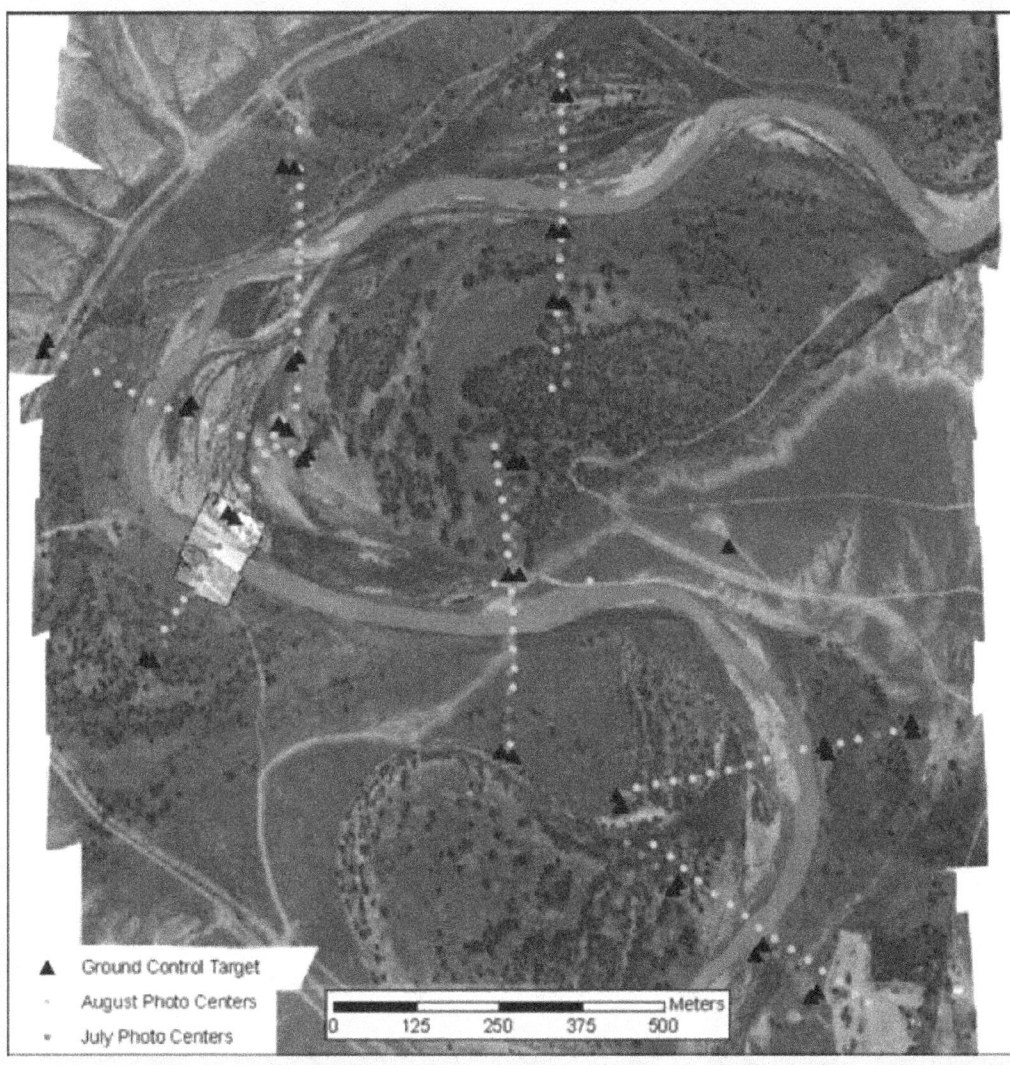

Ground Control Target
August Photo Centers
July Photo Centers

Meters
0   125   250   375   500

Figure 16. Photo targets were placed along selected transects across the Powder River, Wyoming, to assist with geocorrection of large-scale aerial imagery (Noble et al. 2008).

The integration of GPS/IMU systems, VLSA imagery, and CRP techniques hold the potential to greatly expand field sampling intensities, thus enabling more representative coverage of the environmental gradients in the landscape. This will lead to better monitoring information and increased classification accuracies of coarse-scale remote sensing data. Additionally, the integration of these technologies would facilitate the development of proactive monitoring protocols for invasive species.

At all three study sites for which VLSA imagery was obtained, tamarisk *(Tamarix spp.)*—a salt-accumulating, desiccation-tolerant invasive alien species—was shown to have cover values comparable to the native cottonwood *(Populus fremontii)*. Given the high percentage of emergent features of the Powder River channel and the documented tamarisk succession scenarios of other western streams, tamarisk poses an immediate threat to the aquatic habitat and native riparian vegetation. By automatically geocorrecting VLSA imagery using the integration of GPS/IMU systems, great potential for cost-effective monitoring exists. This will allow for the development of protocols for riparian corridors that would enable invasive species to be identified before becoming so infested in an area that management actions become too expensive to implement (Bobo et al. 2008).

Documenting Cultural Resources

The Legend Rock State Archaeological Site enables visitors to view more than 300 petroglyphs spanning a period of thousands of years and representing multiple cultures. Legend Rock, located 28 miles from the town of Thermopolis in north-central Wyoming (Figure 17), was listed on the National Register of Historic Places in 1973 and is world-renowned. A series of sandstone cliffs contain the petroglyphs. Ownership of the cliffs is split among a private land owner, Wyoming State Parks, and the BLM. In 2006, the Legend Rock Interagency Steering Committee was formed. This Committee includes land management agencies, as well as State and local preservation groups and museums. The mission of the Committee is to provide guidance and recommendations to the Wyoming Division of State Parks and Historic Sites on the restoration, maintenance, management, interpretation, promotion, and public accommodation at the Legend Rock State Archaeological Site (Loendorf et al. 2008).

Photogrammetry staff from the NOC was included in the committee from its inception. In fall 2006, NOC staff, accompanied by imaging specialists for Cultural Heritage Imaging, a nonprofit organization that is developing an imaging technique (Mudge et al. 2006) complementary to CRP, joined archaeologists for a visit to the site. This reconnaissance visit provided an opportunity to see and access the site and to determine the approach and resources needed to fully photograph the rock art panels. As a result of the scoping trip, several proof-of-concept 3D image datasets were produced. These virtual 3D models and the CRP techniques were presented at committee meetings, professional archaeological meetings, and for the 2007 Wyoming Joint Senate House Subcommittee on Recreation, Travel, Wildlife, and Cultural Resources. The 3D models provided stunning visualizations of the intricacies and uniqueness of the rock art, offering an early success and a catalyst to energize the committee (Figure 18).

A multiphased approach for documenting the site was developed. During the first phase, a spatially accurate photographic mosaic base map of the sandstone cliff was created. The corrected mosaic, tied to a digital real-world system with RTK GPS, served as base maps for field location,

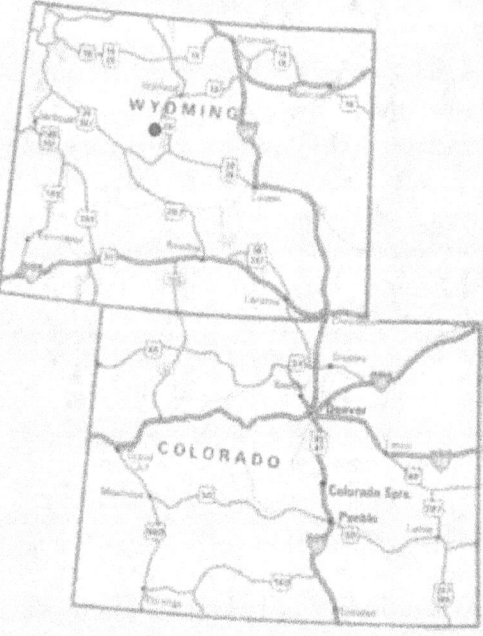

Figure 17. The Legend Rock State Archaeological Site is 28 miles from Thermopolis in north-central Wyoming.

Figure 18. The close-range photogrammetric digital 3D image models can be created and viewed on a laptop computer in the field, providing an on-site demonstration.

inventory, and documentation of rock art panels. The cliff face was photographed from a distance of about 200 m with a 150-mm lens (Figure 19). A resulting resolution and positional accuracy of about 1 cm was achieved (Figure 20). In addition, the digital photo mosaic can be used to provide visual context to more detailed, three-dimensional digital models of individual panels.

The second phase provides detailed three-dimensional modeling and imaging of individual petroglyph panels. The virtual models can be used to record the petroglyphs and to detect even minute changes to the rock art that may occur over time. These highly detailed digital re-creations of the individual panels provide a resolution and accuracy in the tenths of millimeters and provide a baseline for monitoring the site for natural degradation and vandalism. Because of the enormity of the workload for DRS staff, the NOC photogrammetrists provided training in stereoscopic image capture to a State of Wyoming archaeologist involved in the project (Figure 21). In summer 2007, all the

panels on the State-managed land were successfully photographed. In summer 2008, the remaining rock art panels were photographed during a Passport in Time (PIT) project. The PIT program, originated by the Forest Service, allows qualified volunteers to assist in the restoration, recording, and preservation of cultural resource sites. During the 2-week program, photogrammetrists from the NOC provided training in stereoscopic image collection and software processing to the PIT volunteers (Loendorf et al. 2008).

Since the formation of the Legend Rock Interagency Steering Committee, funding for the site has increased, resulting in improvements to infrastructure. An archaeological survey was conducted (Walker et al. 2007) before improvements were made to roads, trails, and parking. The construction of a visitor's center and accommodations for a site host are under way. The photogrammetric documentation will be used as a baseline for inspection and monitoring and for interpretive materials, to include a guide book for the site and interactive digital displays that

Figure 19. The cliff face at Legend Rock State Archaeological Site, Wyoming, was photographed from about 200 m with a 150-mm lens. Inset shows camera orientation and setup.

Figure 20. a. A corrected mosaic of the cliff face at Legend Rock State Archaeological Site, Wyoming, was created by using close-range photogrammetric techniques. b. Close-up view of the mosaic indicated by the black rectangle in a. The pixel resolution of the mosaic is about 1 cm.

incorporate the virtual 3D image models. In addition, the Wyoming Joint Senate House Subcommittee on Recreation, Travel, Wildlife, and Cultural Resources made the preservation and interpretation of Wyoming's cultural resources its first priority for interim study in 2008.

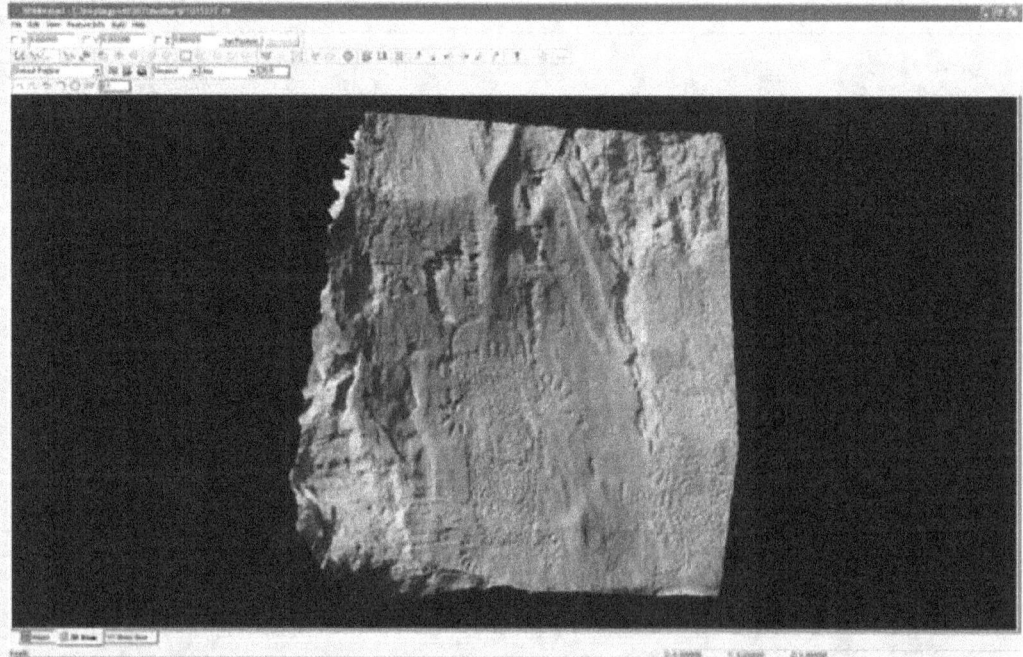

Figure 21. 3D image model of a rock art panel from Legend Rock State Archaeological Site, Wyoming. The stereoscopic images were taken by a State of Wyoming archaeologist during on-site training conducted by photogrammetric staff from the BLM National Operations Center.

CONCLUSION

Documenting and evaluating the condition of its land is a critical part of the Bureau's mission. Condition data obtained by applying photogrammetric techniques provide information on the health of the land and serve as a basis for future decision making; they also provide a tool for determining the effectiveness of present management practices. The availability of digital cameras and the increasing capabilities of computers and analytical software have dramatically expanded the variety of resource applications to which photogrammetry may be applied, while simultaneously decreasing the costs of acquisition, processing, and analysis. The software used to process stereoscopic images to the viewing stage (corrected imagery and 3D surface data) and for use in GIS is presently available within only a few BLM offices. However, the capability to take the needed photographs for close-range photogrammetric projects is not. Field personnel with a vision toward the future will see the value in capturing stereoscopic photographs now. As the types, capability, efficiencies, and availability of 3DMM software increase, these photographs can be used in the future to document changes in condition critical to the Bureau's mission.

The fundamentals of perceiving depth, stereoscopic viewing, and photogrammetry have remained constant through changing technologies. Various 3DMM softwares available on the market today may suggest additional photographs to increase efficiencies. However, the basic geometry will remain the same and allow for measurements to be made from stereoscopic photographs taken 100 years ago, yesterday, or 100 years in the future. Because of this, the concepts of capturing the data and not processing via specific software have been stressed in this document.

The following appendices contain technical information to assist field resource specialists in the successful completion of the imagery collection portion of a basic close-range photogrammetry project. Appendix A outlines the basics of stereoscopic photography. Appendix B discusses the features that should be considered when choosing a camera for CRP documentation. Appendix C discusses factors that can affect picture quality and offers suggestions on taking photographs that will provide successful results. Finally, Appendix D outlines the general steps for conducting the field collection of the photographs for a small CPR project. Also included in Appendix D is an equipment list. When reviewing this list, note that the majority of items (with, perhaps, a few exceptions) are the standard equipment most often taken to the field. That is the benefit of CRP: for the initial field trial of this technology, there is no substantial investment in equipment, only of time— time to read and be familiar with the contents of this document and time to practice taking the needed photographs in the field.

A fixed grid of varying height was used as an early method of providing x,y, and z control at the Red Gulch Dinosaur Tracksite in Wyoming.

REFERENCES

Birch, J. S. 2006. Using 3DM Analyst Mine Mapping Suite for rock face characterisation. *In* F. Tonon and J. Kottenstette, editors. Laser and Photogrammetric Methods for Rock Face Characterization.

Bobo, M., T. Booth, S. Cox, N. Matthews, R. McDougal, G. Meyer, and T. Noble. 2008. Application of high resolution remote sensing for monitoring aquatic and riparian habitats within the Powder River Basin in Wyoming. *In* 12th Biennial USDA Forest Service Remote Sensing Applications Conference RS-2008. [abstracts and program]

Breithaupt, B. H., and N. A. Matthews. 2004. An integrated approach to three-dimensional data collection at dinosaur tracksites in the Rocky Mountain West. Ichnos 11(1–2):11.

Forbes, K., A..Voigt, and N. Bodika. 2002. An inexpensive, automatic, and accurate camera calibration method. *In* Proceedings of the Thirteenth Annual Symposium of the Pattern Recognition Association of South Africa.

Hussain, M., and J. Bethel. 2004. Project and mission planning. *In* J. C. McGlone, editor, Manual of Photogrammetry, 5th edition. American Society for Photogrammetry and Remote Sensing. 1151 pp.

Loendorf, L., and C. McClellan. 2008. Management of Legend Rock Archaeological Site. Paper presented at the Binational Petroglyph Conference, Albuquerque, New Mexico, September 2007.

Matthews, N. A., T. A. Noble, and B. H. Breithaupt. 2004. Page 348 *in* Dinosaur tracks to dam faces: A new method for collecting three-dimensional data. Geological Society of America Abstracts 36(5).

Matthews, N. A., T. A. Noble, and B. H. Breithaupt. 2006. The application of photogrammetry, remote sensing, and geographic information systems (GIS) to fossil resource management. Pages 119–131 *in* S. G. Lucas, J. A. Spielmann, P. M. Hester, J. P. Kenworthy, and V. L. Santucci, editors. Fossils from Federal Lands. New Mexico Museum of Natural History and Science Bulletin 34.

Matthews, N. A., T. A. Noble, M. Bies, L. Loendorf, D. N. Walker, M. Mudge, and C. McClellan. 2007. Photographing the past, protecting the future: Using close-range photogrammetry to capture 3D images of the Legend Rock Petroglyph Site, WY. *In* 34th Annual Meeting of the American Rock Art Research Association, Abstracts and Program. La Pinta 33(4).

Matthews, N. A., T. A. Noble, W. G. Ypsilantis, and D. Murphy. 2007. Of time and the soil: Detecting microtopographic changes using extreme close-range photogrammetry.

Mudge, M., T. Malzbender, C. Schroer, and L. Marlin. 2006. New reflection transformation imaging methods for rock art and multiple-viewpoint display. *In* M. Ioannides, D. Arnold, F. Niccolucci, and K. Mania, editors. Proceedings of the Seventh International Symposium on Virtual Reality, Archaeology, and Cultural Heritage (VAST2007). Eurographics Association.

Noble, T. A., and N. A. Matthews. 2007. A new look at capturing detailed 3D images of rock art: Advances in close-range photogrammetry. *In* 34th Annual Meeting of the American Rock Art Research Association. La Pinta 33(4). [abstracts and program]

Noble, T. A., N. A. Matthews, T. Booth, S. Cox, and M. Bobo. 2008. Application of close-range photogrammetric techniques to Very Large Scale Aerial (VLSA) Photography for monitoring aquatic and riparian habitats. *In* 12th Biennial USDA Forest Service Remote Sensing Applications Conference RS-2008. [abstracts and program]

Walker, D. N., M. Bovee, M. Karnopp, and T. Noble. 2007. Archaeological Investigations and Rock Art Recording at Legend Rock State Archaeological Site, Wyoming. *In* 65th Annual Plains Anthropological Conference Abstracts.

Ypsilantis, W. G., T. Noble, and N. Matthews. 2007. OHV Use Monitoring with Extreme Close-Range Photogrammetry. Project report to the BLM Field Office in Montrose, Colorado. Bureau of Land Management, National Science and Technology Center, Denver, Colorado. 6 pp. [unpublished]

APPENDIX A
CONCEPTS OF STEREOSCOPIC PHOTOGRAPHY

Stereoscopic photographs are taken to mimic the three-dimensional viewing capability resulting from the offset of a person's left and right eyes (Figure A.1). The first consideration when designing the stereophoto layout is the needed precision (scale) that is required to adequately represent the subject. As in traditional film photogrammetry, the scale has a geometric relationship between the height of the sensor and the focal length of the lens (Hussain and Bethel 2004).

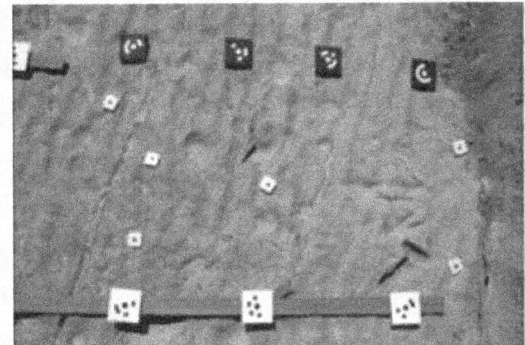 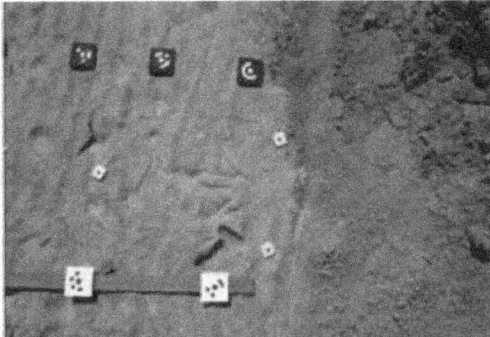

Figure A.1. Stereoscopic photograph pairs of a dinosaur track from the Red Gulch Dinosaur Tracksite, Wyoming.

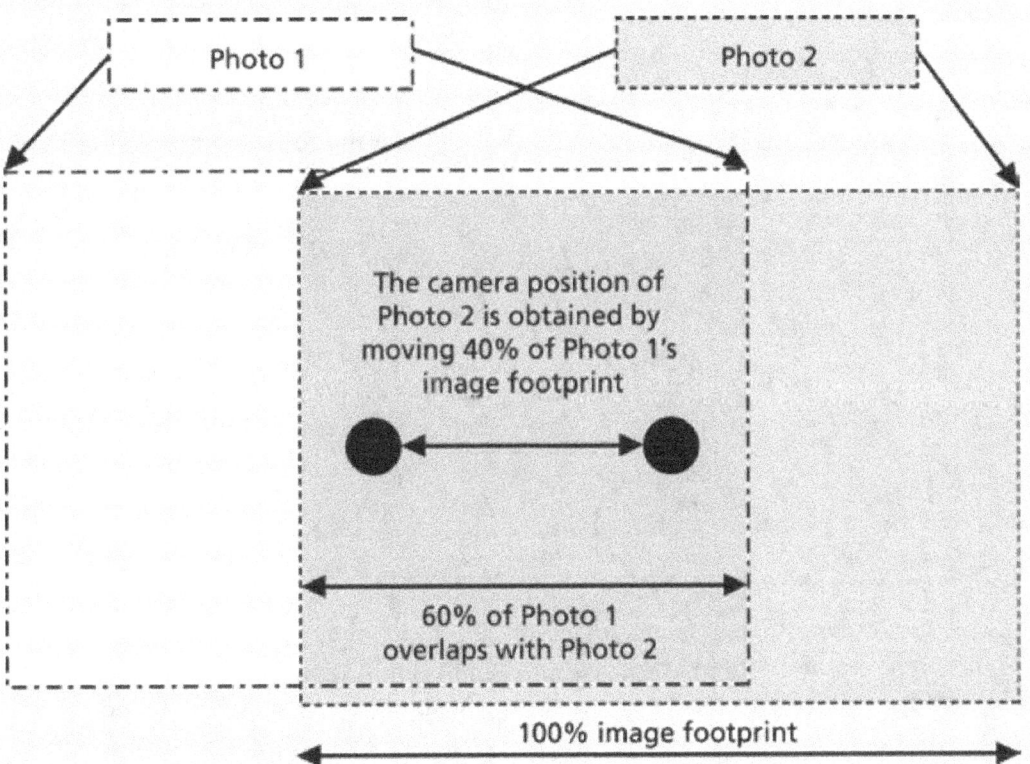

Figure A.2. The large black dots represent photo centers and thus the camera position. A dashed rectangle is associated with each photo center dot and represents the field of view, or footprint, of that image. The best stereophoto pairs overlap each other by 60%. This is achieved by actually moving the camera position of each photo by 40% of the photo's footprint.

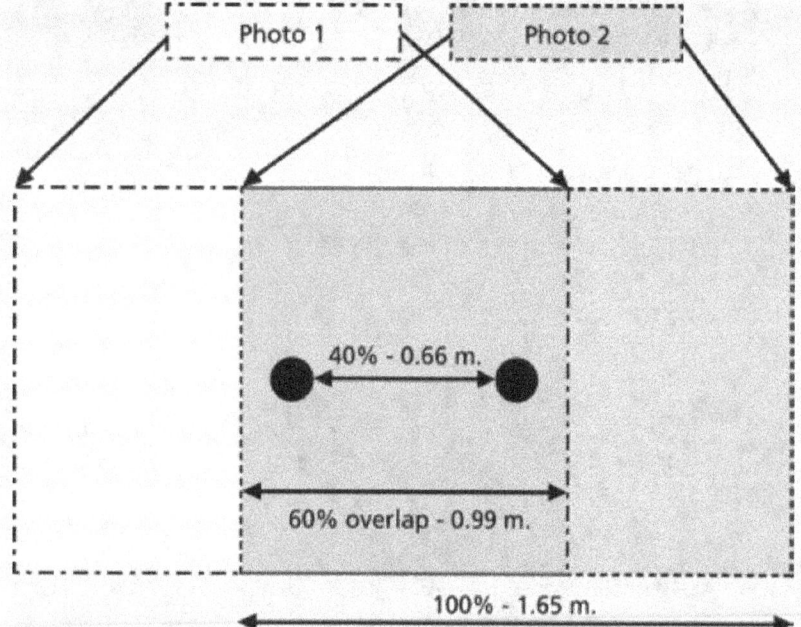

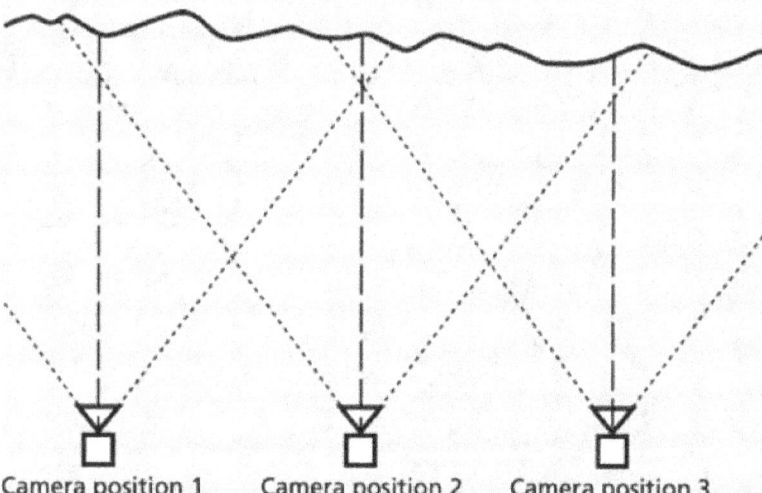

Figure A.3. In this example, each image footprint is 1.65 m, thus the amount of stereoscopic overlap (at 60%) is 0.99 m (0.60 × 1.65 = 0.99). To achieve 60% overlap, the camera must be moved by 40% of the image footprint, which is 0.66 m (1.65 × 0.4 = 0.66).

Figure A.4. Graphic of parallel images with typically 60% overlap (Birch 2006). An imaginary ray (dashed line) drawn through the center of the lens should be as perpendicular to the plane of the subject as possible. All images are taken with one camera that is moved in sequence from position one to two, to three, and so forth.

$$\text{scale} = \frac{\text{focal length}}{\text{height above terrain}}$$

For example: $\dfrac{6 \text{ inches (0.5 feet)}}{2,000 \text{ feet}} = 0.00025$

$$1/0.00025 = 4,000$$

$$\text{Scale} = 1{:}4{,}000$$

The pixel resolution, or Sensor Pixel Size (SPS), of a commercial digital camera can be factored into the preceding equation to determine the ground resolution, or ground sample distance (GSD), of the resulting image. The SPS is computed by taking the physical width of the sensor divided by the width of the sensor in pixels.

$$GSD = SPS * H / f$$

where SPS is the Sensor Pixel Size (in micrometers),
H is the camera height, or distance from the object (in meters), and
f is the focal length of the lens (in millimeters).
GSD will be in meters; multiply by 1,000 for GSD in millimeters

The best stereophoto pairs have an overlap of 60% (Figure A.2). Once the desired GSD is determined, the camera height and distance between camera stations can be calculated.

For example, when using a 10 megapixel SLR with a sensor size of 23.6 × 15.8 mm and pixel dimensions of 3,872 × 2,592, the SPS = 23.6 / 3,872 = 0.00610 mm. Therefore, with a 20-mm lens, and shooting at a height of 1.4 m above the subject, the GSD—is 0.43 mm. The area covered (or footprint) of each photo would be 1.65 × 1.11 m. For a 60% overlap, the distance between camera stations is 0.66 m, which is 40% of the image footprint (Figure A.3).

A simple way to determine the image footprint in the field is to mark points on the ground on either side of the frame of the viewfinder when the camera is at the appropriate distance from the subject. Then measure the distance between these points and calculate 40% of that distance.

The orientation of the camera or sensor to the subject is also an important consideration. It is most desirable to have imagery that is taken as close to nadir—that is, with the camera perpendicular to the subject—as possible. A tripod (with an extension arm when shooting down) can greatly aid in positioning the lens directly over the subject (Figure A.4). This also positions the plane of the sensor parallel to the subject and helps to reduce perspective distortions in the image (Figure A.5).

In some instances, nadir photography is not practical because of constraints imposed by the terrain or project size. In such instances, oblique photography must be used.

Photographs deviating significantly from nadir that have a high angle to the object are referred to as high-angle oblique photos (Figure A.6a). When nadir photos are not a practical option, high-angle oblique

Figure A.5. It is important for the camera to maintain a consistent relation to the subject. Keeping a perpendicular angle to the subject is preferable. The dashed line represents the ray described in Appendix Figure A.4. A tripod with an extension arm was used when photographing a dinosaur trackway at the Red Gulch Dinosaur Tracksite, Wyoming.

photos are preferred for several reasons: ability to get closer to the subject while still filling the frame, stronger angles for resolving the 3D coordinate positions, and less distortion of features.

Photographs taken at a low angle to the subject are referred to as low-angle oblique photos (Figure A.6b). Low-angle oblique photos are not desirable, as both the subject and control targets can be highly distorted. However, if an in situ object is being photographed and low-angle oblique photos are the only option, they may be used. With experience and care, low-angle oblique photos may successfully be used for measurement.

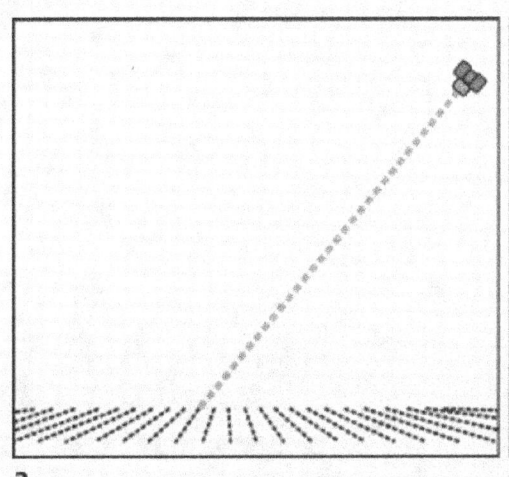

a.

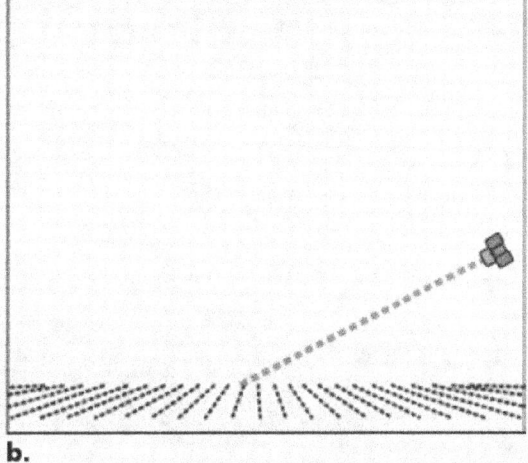

b.

Figure A.6. A line of sight not directly nadir (perpendicular) to the subject is considered oblique. a. Photos taken at a high-angle oblique camera angle can be used when needed and will provide successful results. b. Photos taken when the line of sight to the subject is sharp (a low-angle oblique camera angle), should be avoided unless absolutely necessary to provide stereo overlap.

Extending the reach to photograph a difficult to access rock art panel in the Bighorn Basin of Wyoming.

CHOOSING A CAMERA

Digital cameras and 3DMM software have most certainly revolutionized the CRP process. Previously, an expensive metric or surveying camera was required. These cameras are equipped with required fixed-focus lenses with predetermined focal distances and are manufactured to a high level of precision and stability. However, even with care in manufacturing, lens distortions could not be completely eliminated and a manufacturer's calibration report would accompany each camera. The calibration report includes the size of the frame, location of any fiducials, the focal length, principal point, and distortion co-efficients of the camera–lens system. The information from the calibration report is used in setting up the stereo model so that the resulting measurements could be made without the effects of distortion from the camera–lens system.

Now the 3DMM software allows us to exploit the ever-increasing number of digital cameras on the market today. The main reason for this is that the 3DMM provides a camera calibration function. This not only removes the restriction of using an expensive metric camera, but also allows for the ad hoc calibration of most camera–lens systems. This is exciting, as it provides for the capability to increase the ground sample distance (GSD) as cameras come on the market with improved sensors. However, it also makes it difficult to suggest a particular camera, as innovations seem to occur frequently. It is important to note that, whereas a digital SLR camera is suggested, successful projects can be ac-complished with a point-and-shoot camera. Thus, the following recommendations highlight features to consider when choosing a camera for CRP documentation.

Resolution

The final accuracy of your measurements and resulting terrain surface are governed by the resolution, or GSD, of the stereo-scopic images of your subject. The GSD is governed by the resolution of the camera sensor (higher is better), the focal length of the lens, and the distance from the subject (closer is better). The resolution of the images is governed by the number of pixels per given area and the size of the sensor. A 6 megapixel resolution generally provides good results for a variety of subjects. However, an 8 to 10 megapixel resolution provides much more flexibility and achieves higher accuracies. The sensor size does have to be considered along with the resolution. The conventional way to categorize digital camera sensor size is similar to the sizing of television screens; that is, dimensions are given across the diagonal. The ratio of the sensor is often compared to the 35-mm film that it has replaced (43.3 mm diagonal). The sensor does have a bearing on image quality, with the 28.4 mm sensor found in most digital SLR cameras having the best quality. The sensors of midrange cameras are often 11.0 mm, whereas those of compact digital cameras are 6.72 mm. These smaller sensors can introduce noise in the image. Thus, a compact digital camera with a 1/2.7-inch sensor, even at 12 megapixels, would produce a less desirable image than one with a 11.0 mm sensor, at 8 megapixels.

Lens Flexibility

The length of the lens directly affects the field of view (the base-to-height ratio, the distance from an object and, finally, the accuracy and number of photos needed to cover a subject). Shorter lenses (18 to 30 mm) provide the widest field of view and are good for capturing a subject from close distances with a minimal number of photographs. Longer lenses (100 to 300 mm) are excellent for capturing a subject from greater distances but provide a narrower field of view. However, it can be expensive to have a variety of fixed-length lenses on hand.

Many digital SLR cameras are sold in a "kit" with a compound zoom lens. A fixed-focus lens will always produce a higher quality image; however, the kit lenses are good in that they provide versatility and can reduce start-up costs. Successful CRP projects can be accomplished with zoom lenses when special care is taken.

Manual Focus

Ensuring that a series of stereophotos are captured at the same focal distance is vital to the successful completion of a project. The capability to "take control" of the focus from the camera is accomplished by the manual focus setting. Most SLR and midrange consumer cameras have this capability. The manual focus setting helps to ensure that each photo in the stereo sequence is taken with the same focal distance (although autofocus can be used as long as a constant distance between the camera and the subject is maintained).

Aperture Priority

The aperture setting not only determines the amount of light that reaches the sensor but also controls the depth of field (the point at which the image begins to blur). Thus, it is necessary to use a camera for which the aperture can take priority over the other settings that affect the lighting, such as shutter speed or ISO (International Organization for Standardization; *http://www.dpreview.com/learn/?/Glossary/Digital_Imaging*). Although this feature is standard on digital SLR cameras, it may not be available on compact cameras.

Image Format

There are a number of different digital image formats. Each format has advantages and disadvantages based on the use and type of compression. Digital image files that are unprocessed, or RAW, contain the original information from the sensor and capture a greater bit depth than other standard formats. The RAW images must be processed in some type of image manipulation software, which often comes with the camera, or third party software such as Adobe Photoshop. The ability to manipulate the RAW image provides for the opportunity to make some exposure corrections after the photos are taken and may allow for the extraction of detail in areas of deep shadow. Other types of image files, such as .jpg (Joint Photographic Experts Group) and .tif (Tagged Image File Format), are processed within the camera and will not provide the same amount of flexibility in post processing (*http://www.dpreview.com/learn/?/Glossary/Digital_Imaging*). Cameras that capture images in RAW file format, or a combination of .jpg and RAW, are preferred.

Lens Distortion

All camera lens systems have distortions because of the curvature of the lens and the alignment of the lens with the sensor. To quantify these distortions and effectively remove them, 3DMM software provides camera calibration functions as part of the project work-flow (Figure B.1). The additional images needed for the camera calibration can be easily integrated into the stereoscopic workflow and are discussed in Appendix C.

The following cameras have been successfully used within the BLM for CRP projects: Canon Powershot A640; Olympus C8080 and EV500; Nikon D70, D80, D200, and D3; and Canon 5D and 1D.

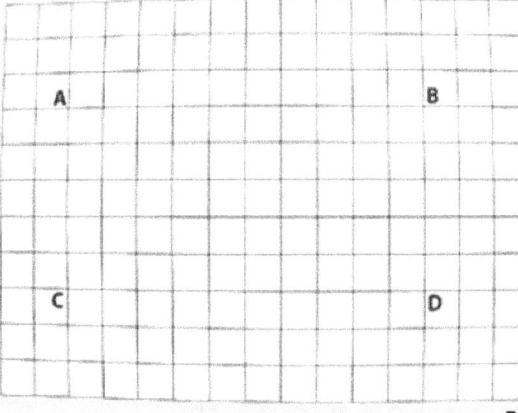

Figure B.1. a. Photograph of a straight-line rectangular grid. The curvature of the lines is due to the most common type of lens distortion, which is barrel distortion.

a.

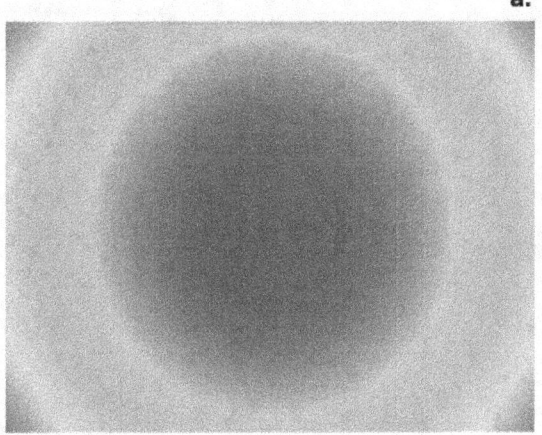

b. Graphic representation of lens distortion. The least distorted portion of the lens is in the center (depicted in blue). During the camera calibration process, the focal length, format size, principal point, and distortion coefficients (K_1, K_2, K_3, P_1, and P_2) of the camera-lens system are calculated.

b.

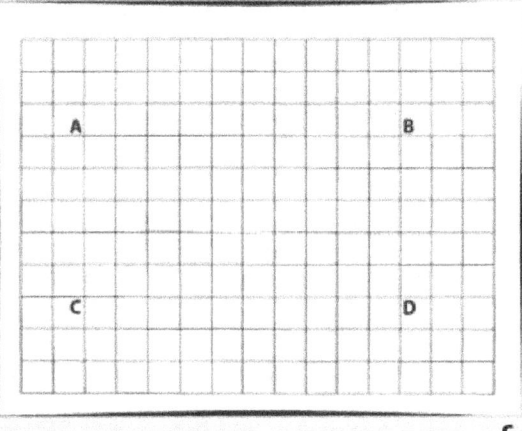

c. The corrected photograph from a. after the lens distortion parameters were applied. The results can be seen in the straightening of the grid lines and a visible change of the image.

c.

Due to the minimal equipment requirements of close-range photogrammetry, subjects in difficult terrain, such as this area north of Albuquerque, New Mexico, can be documented more readily.

APPENDIX C
TAKING GOOD PICTURES AND SUGGESTED CAMERA SETTINGS

The crucial element to a successful close-range photogrammetric process is attaining "good" photographs. In this instance, the term good refers to a series of pictures that have uniform exposure and are high-contrast, sharp images that fill the frame with the subject. Close-range photographs may never appear on the cover of *National Geographic* magazine or thrill your friends and neighbors, but they must be of sufficient quality that the autocorrelation function of the 3DMM software can function properly.

Environmental factors, the camera used, and the experience of the photographer all contribute to the success of the CRP project. The following section offers recommendations for composing your photos and correctly adjusting the camera settings. It is important to have adequate experience with the camera you are using and be able to adjust it to meet the circumstances. If you can operate your camera and understand the techniques for capturing CRP, you will be able to document, in measurable 3D, almost any subject at almost any time, just with a camera and your brain.

Taking Good Pictures

Several requirements must be met when taking photos suitable for photogrammetry. Every photo needs to be clear, properly exposed, and have adequate overlap with adjacent photos (Appendix A).

Lighting is one of the most critical factors in taking good CRP photographs, and perhaps one of the most difficult to control. The 3DMM autocorrelation process works very well for properly illuminated, high-contrast areas. However, areas of low contrast and uniform color, areas with high relief displacement, or areas that are obscured (by deep shadows or other features) can lead to mismatching and poor terrain correlation. One of the biggest causes of poor photos is inconsistent light caused by shadows. Shadows can be created by features of the subject that you are documenting or cast by features outside the area of interest (such as your head). When photographing out-of-doors, choose a time of day when shadows are minimal. This may occur when the sun is directly overhead. The resulting photographs may not emphasize the subject visually; however, properly exposed images taken in full sun have outstanding results during autocorrelation. Use proper camera settings to ensure photographs taken during full sun are not overexposed. Other times of consistent lighting can occur on overcast or cloudy days, or when the subject is in full shadow. In these instances, it may be necessary to slow the shutter speed or use a tripod to ensure that photographs are not underexposed. Keep in mind that lighting and weather conditions can change quickly.

When shooting indoors, make sure the area is as well lighted as possible. Take a few test shots and examine them to make sure that images are not underexposed or blurry. Indoor illumination can be a problem and it may be necessary to slow the shutter speed or use a tripod to ensure that photographs are properly exposed. Using the flash function of the camera is not a good option, as it can cast odd shadows and flares that fall differently through successive stereo pairs, thus affecting autocorrelation. However, stationary light sources such as floodlights, which evenly illuminate the subject, may be necessary in very low light conditions. When setting up lighting, make sure to provide adequate room around the subject for taking a complete set of stereophotos.

Filling the frame with the subject is also crucial. For small CRP projects, it may be most straightforward to observe the subject through the viewfinder to best determine camera height and overlap. When photographing a larger project or when oblique orientations are necessary, remember to center your subject in the frame. There is often no need to ensure the horizon or other points of reference are in every frame, especially if they detract from the subject that is being documented.

Camera Settings

The 3DMM software used for close-range photogrammetry documentation supports a great variety of cameras. Therefore, it is beyond the scope of this document to list each setting on each camera that could possibly be used for CRP documentation. The following should serve as a general checklist and reminder of settings to check for and should aid in avoiding pitfalls. However, it is important that the operator be familiar with the camera to be used for CRP and with the results that will be produced as settings are manipulated.

Focal Length and Distance

The settings that most dramatically affect success of the CRP project are the focal length (lens or zoom length) and focus distance. A fixed focal length lens makes this process most efficient; however, the zoom capability of multifocal length lenses can be an asset in variable field conditions as the camera lens system may be zoomed or focused to any setting that is appropriate for capturing project detail. However, it is necessary to perform the camera calibration and conduct the project at the same focal length and focus distance. A streamlined

approach for multifocal length lenses is to zoom to either the minimum or maximum extent of the lens and set the focal distance to infinity. Use tape with a minimal amount of residue, such as painters tape, to fix the lens in position.

For cameras that allow the operator to switch freely between autofocus and manual focus, the following produces effective results: Hold the camera at the height or distance at which you will be shooting or mount it on the tripod. Turn the control to autofocus and take a shot. Check that the distance registered on the lens is accurate and check the LCD (Liquid Crystal Display), or download the image to make sure it is in focus. Then switch to manual focus and tape the lens ring to make sure it does not move for the session in which you will be shooting at that constant distance.

Focus Weighting

Many cameras allow you to dictate how the appropriate focus is determined. For example, the camera may take readings from the center of the field of view, average readings from a number of locations, or take continuous readings. It is important to take several test shots and vary the mode of determining the autofocus to ensure that the appropriate focus is achieved for a particular situation.

Aperture

Set the camera on aperture priority. An aperture of f8 (or 35 mm equivalent) is recommended for CRP, as this provides a good depth of field. Proper depth of field ensures that the entire subject is in good focus, which is important for image matching. When shooting at a close distance to the subject, it may be necessary to increase the aperture to f11 or stop down the aperture to get the best depth of field. Refer to your camera manual or digital photography guide for a thorough discussion of aperture and depth of field.

"Film" Speed

The sensitivity of the sensor to light is defined by the International Organization for Standardization (ISO; *http://www.dpreview.com/learn/?/Glossary/Digital_Imaging*). The ISO setting affects the amount of light that the sensor will absorb during a defined period. The ISO range of a camera is dependent on a number of factors and it is helpful to consult the camera manual when setting the ISO. In general, the brighter the lighting conditions the lower the ISO. When shooting outside on a bright, sunny day, an ISO of 100 (or even lower if supported by the camera) is appropriate. In low-light situations, it may be necessary to increase the ISO to compensate for the aperture setting of f8. It is possible to get graininess or artifacts when the ISO has been pushed too high. Testing for the optimum ISO is important in low-light conditions.

Shutter Speed

While the shutter speed will be determined automatically by the camera once the aperture and ISO have been set, it is a good idea to be aware of the shutter speed. A shutter speed of at least 1/200th of a second is required for handheld photography. For lower shutter speed, adjusting the ISO or mounting the camera on a tripod may be necessary. Should there be camera motion from the wind or an unstable platform (such as a ladder), high shutter speeds (more than 1/1,000th of a second) may be necessary.

File Format

If possible, set to a combination of RAW + FINE. If not, set the file format to RAW if available; otherwise, set to the highest quality .tif or .jpg possible.

Image Rotation

Turn this setting off. The photo orientation must be known with respect to the camera and lens. Automatic image rotation will rotate the image 90° clockwise or counter-clockwise. At first, this may not seem like it would cause a problem, but experience has shown otherwise. When taking nadir photos, it is sometimes impossible to tell which way the camera was rotated when the picture was taken. This can easily happen if photos are taken on opposite sides of a subject with no horizon in the view. The camera calibration cannot be applied correctly if the original orientation is not known.

File Naming

Most digital cameras provide the option to customize the file name or numbering template. Two basic options are the continuous numeric incrementing of file names and restarting the numbering sequence each time the memory card is reinserted. Consecutive numbering is the best option, as it helps to ensure that image files are not overwritten during download. In addition, duplicate file names may be a problem when processing several sequences of images together in the same project.

Custom Settings

As digital cameras advance, so do the options for settings that are tailored to a specific brand of camera. These settings include auto sharpening, white balance, vibrating of the sensor to dislodge dust particles, and others. Once again, it is strongly recommended that time is taken to experiment with how each of these settings, will affect image quality and usability in a CRP project. In most instances (especially image sharpening, stabilization, and sensor vibration for cleaning), it is important to turn off these options.

Objects of known length, with circles at a calibrated distance and circular barcodes, surround a 1-meter-square area of biological soil crust in the Dry Creek Basin near Montrose, Colorado.

Appendix D
Conducting a CRP Project

To take useable stereophotos, some procedures must be followed. By adhering to these procedures, quality photos and efficient processing of those photos is ensured. In general, the steps to be followed are the same regardless of the camera or subject being photographed. However, certain circumstances will require flexibility and ingenuity, which comes with experience.

Close-Range Photogrammetry (CRP) projects can be placed into one of two categories—small (simple) and large (complex). Large projects are those with an area of interest greater than 5 m² or where complexities of terrain or access add to the level of expertise needed for planning and execution of the project. Projects that fall into this category may require a preliminary site visit or the inspection of overview photographs taken of the area. In some instances, the needed vantage points for capturing imagery may not be present, necessitating alternatives to ground-based capture, such as the use of a large ladder, aerial blimp, unmanned aerial system, or other type of elevated platform. Whereas the same basic procedures and equipment apply to both small and large projects, it would be difficult to address all the complexities that could arise with large projects and is beyond the scope of this document.

Small projects have an area of interest equivalent to or smaller than about 5 m². This type of project may also be referred to as extreme close-range as high precision of data points is expected. Design and image acquisition for small projects may be successfully carried out by resource specialists in the field. An overview of the procedures for small or extreme CRP will be provided in this appendix.

Project Planning

The first step in project planning is to establish the need for capturing 3D data of a subject and the detail and accuracy at which the data must be captured. Because of the versatility of the CRP process, the images needed for 3DMM process can be easily captured. This provides great flexibility in the subjects and uses for 3D data. Examples of data capture and use include the establishment of plots for vegetation or erosion monitoring, baseline capture of a feature, taking measurements of a delicate subject that can (or should) not be touched, and dense surface capture for hardcopy reproduction.

Because of the flexibility of the CRP technique, it is possible to obtain high accuracy 3D data from subjects that are at almost any orientation with respect to the camera position. Documentation can be conducted looking straight down at the ground, looking straight ahead at a rock art panel or historical structure, looking at a hillside from an oblique angle, or looking overhead. In all these instances, the same basic principles apply. It is important to get the plane of the sensor and lens parallel to the subject, to maintain a consistent height (or distance) from the subject, to ensure the subject has consistent illumination, and to make sure there is an object of known length in at least three images. To streamline the following discussion, it will be assumed that the camera is facing straight down at the subject. If this is not the situation, camera distance can be interchanged for camera height.

In general, the subject of 3D documentation falls into one of two categories based on the size of the feature to be captured.

Either it is small enough that it may be captured in its entirety (such as a rock art panel) or it is so large that only samples of the area can be economically captured (such as soil erosion monitoring plots). These subjects are referred to as predetermined and sample, respectively. Predetermined subjects are specific features that are to be documented, such as a dinosaur track, historical structure, specific erosional feature, or something specific that must be measured. Sample features refer to situations where there is a defined area to be studied, but the exact site of the CRP project can be selected within that area. An example would be the establishment of a plot for erosion, vegetation, or other types of monitoring. The following section makes recommendations for establishing a sample monitoring plot.

Sample Plot Establishment

For areas as large as 5 m², stereoscopic images with a GSD of 0.5 mm are easily achievable. For most applications, this would provide a suitable level of 3D documentation. It is, therefore, necessary to determine the size of the plot. Depending on the study to be undertaken, the size can vary from 0.5 × 0.5 m² to a rectangular area of 1.0 × 5.0 m. It is recommended that sites be selected with different geomorphic characteristics. Keep in mind that vegetation can have an effect on the density of 3D data collection. This can result from plant movement caused by wind during successive stereophoto acquisition or by simply obscuring the ground. Choosing a site with minimal vegetation would be optimal; however, information may be gained by selecting sites with varying vegetation types, heights, and percentages of ground cover.

Choose a location where the effect on the site can be limited. Try not to step or walk within the sample area, especially if the activity will affect the results of the study. If the CRP is going to be repeated over successive intervals, it is important to place monuments, such as survey nails or rebar (if appropriate), at the four corners of the site and at least one additional point in the middle of each side, for a total of six monuments. Longer plots should have additional monuments along the sides (one every 1.5 m is suggested). The monuments should be driven flush to the ground to minimize movement. File the top of the rebar to smooth the top surface and the edges. Make sure the top of the rebar is as smooth as possible. Monuments should have a small center point punched into them for exact positioning or marking. It is important that the monument be visible in the stereo sequence. To ensure ease of location it is helpful to place a circular object over the rebar. A compact disk (CD) that has been spray-painted white works very well. It is important to ensure that the rebar used is small enough to fit snugly inside of the hole in the CD. If a number of plots are to be established, it is important to consider both the amount of time required to travel between sites, as well as setup time.

Predetermined Sites

For projects in which the subject is predetermined, the size of the area to photograph will be dictated by the extent of the feature. Deviations from this may occur when the feature is larger than 5 m², and only a portion of it will be documented. In this instance, it is necessary to choose an area that will provide the most representative information for the entire site. Although the long-term goal of the documentation may be monitoring, it is not always permissible to mark many subjects (such as cultural resources) with a monument. In these instances, selecting unique, photoidentifiable natural features as reference points may be necessary, and the use of high-accuracy GPS to relocate established control points over time may be required.

Photo Layout

Once the size and area of interest have been established, the next step is to determine the most effective photo layout. It is important to strike a balance between the level of resolution needed, completely covering the area with overlapping stereophotos, setup time, and processing time. Two approaches can be taken—one minimizes the number of photos needed and the other sets out to achieve a particular resolution.

Several examples (Figures D.1, D.2, and D.3) illustrate the layouts that can be used for CRP, including single strip and block layouts. When preplanning a photo layout or doing so on an ad hoc basis in the field, it is important to maintain a consistent height and 60% overlap for good stereoscopic photographs (see Appendix A).

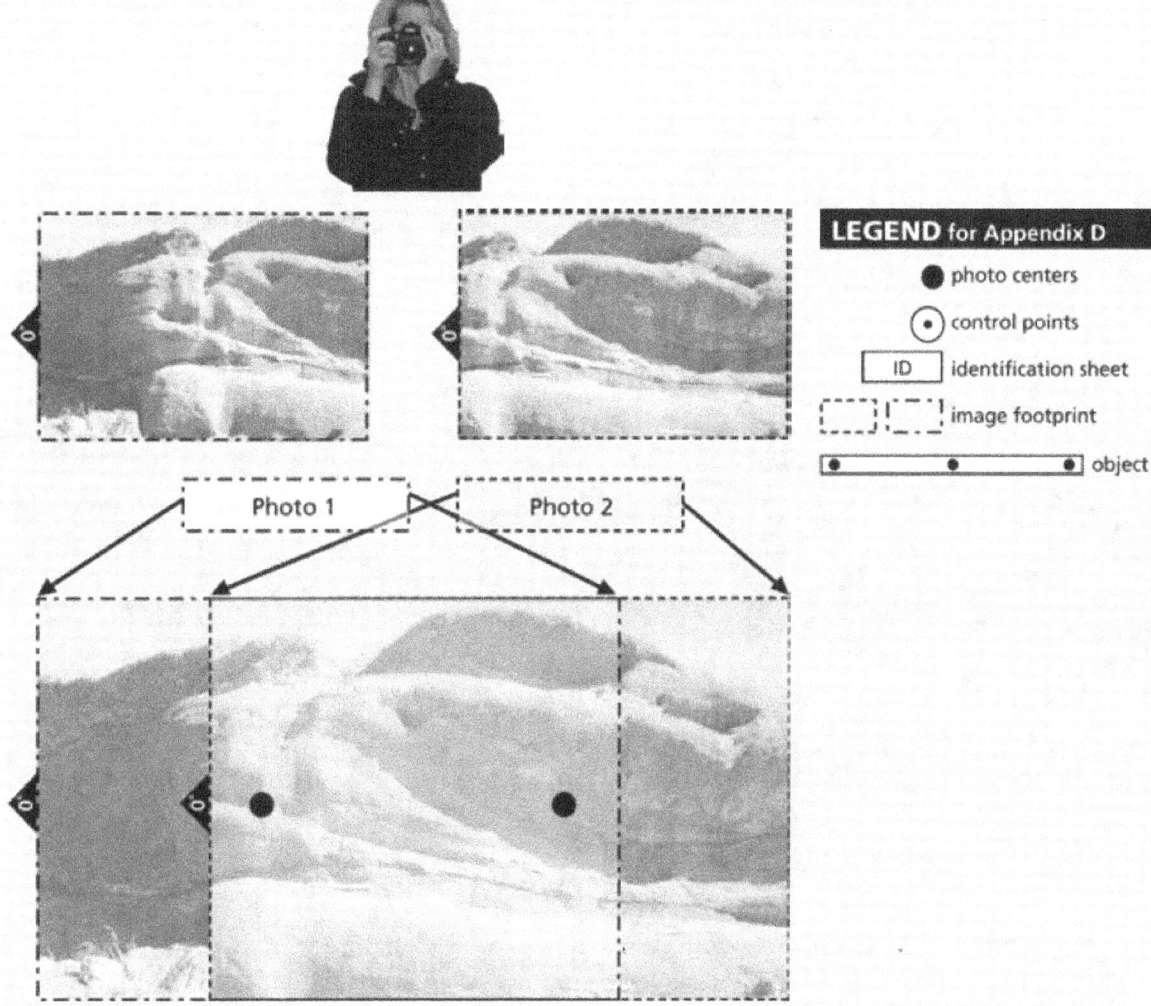

LEGEND for Appendix D

- ● photo centers
- ⊙ control points
- [ID] identification sheet
- ⌐ ¬ image footprint
- ●————●————● object of known length

Photo 1   Photo 2

Figure D.1. A small subject requiring a single stereo pair. When needed, an identification (ID) sheet can be placed in the first frame of the stereo sequence, to the left of the area of interest. ID sheets are helpful when photographing a series of subjects that have reference identification codes, such as monitoring plot numbers or museum catalogue codes. The date, weather conditions, photographer, and other types of information can be added to the ID sheet.

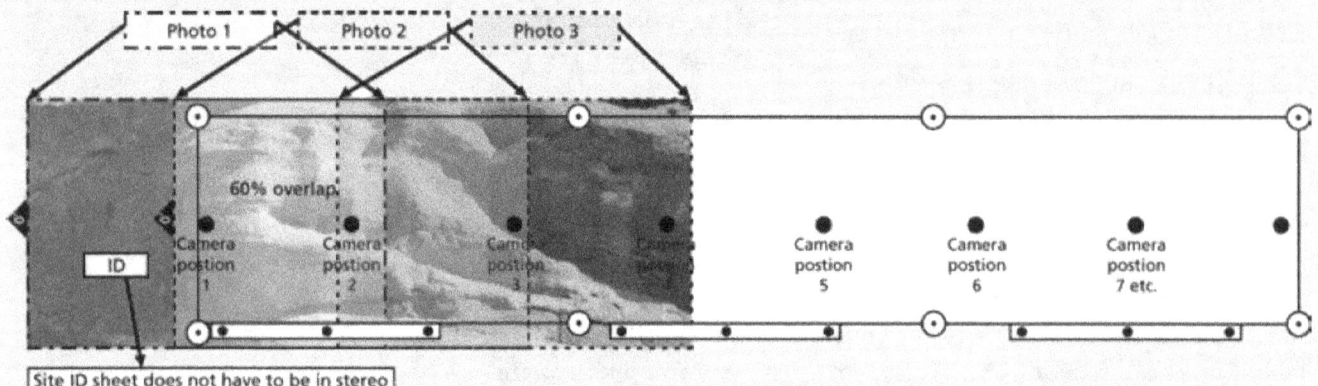

Figure D.2. Photo layout for a single strip of overlapping stereoscopic photography. A single camera is used to photograph each image in succession by moving from one camera position to the next. Note that control points are only necessary when tying photographs to an established reference, such as real-world coordinates or a monitoring datum. An object of known length or calibrated control stick is always necessary.

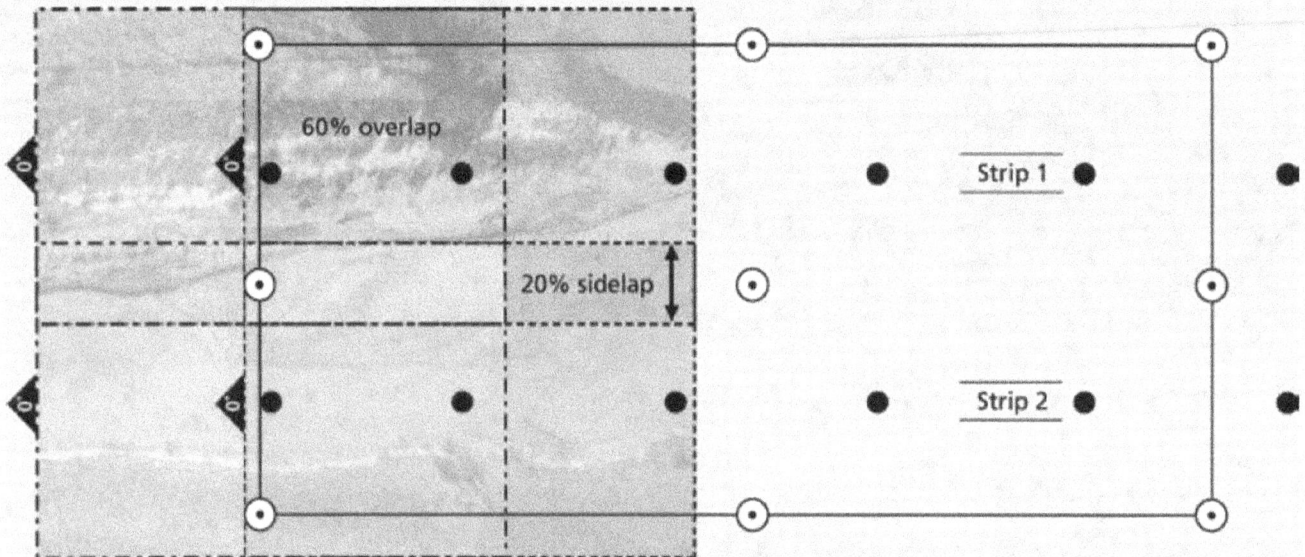

Figure D.3. In some instances, the size of the subject may dictate that two or more lines, or strips, of photography are needed to completely capture the subject in stereo. In these instances, a block approach is taken. For a block it is necessary to maintain about 20% sidelap between strips. Control points in the sidelap area are useful. This figure uses low-level aerial images from the Powder River Monitoring project to illustrate overlap and sidelap for block setup.

Camera Calibration

Camera calibration photographs must be captured at the same settings as the stereophotos. This can be achieved by simply taking at least two additional photos turned 90° to the previous photos and two additional photos turned 270° to the previous photos (Figure D.4). This is easily accomplished by adding two additional photographs at the beginning or end of the stereo shots. The main purpose of the camera calibration is to determine and map the distortions in the lens with respect to the sensor location. The software accomplishes this most effectively when there are a large number of autocorrelated points in common between the stereoscopic images and the additional 90° and 270° photos (Figures D.5 and D.6). In some instances (such as a strip of only a few models), it may be desirable to recapture the entire strip at 90° and 270°.

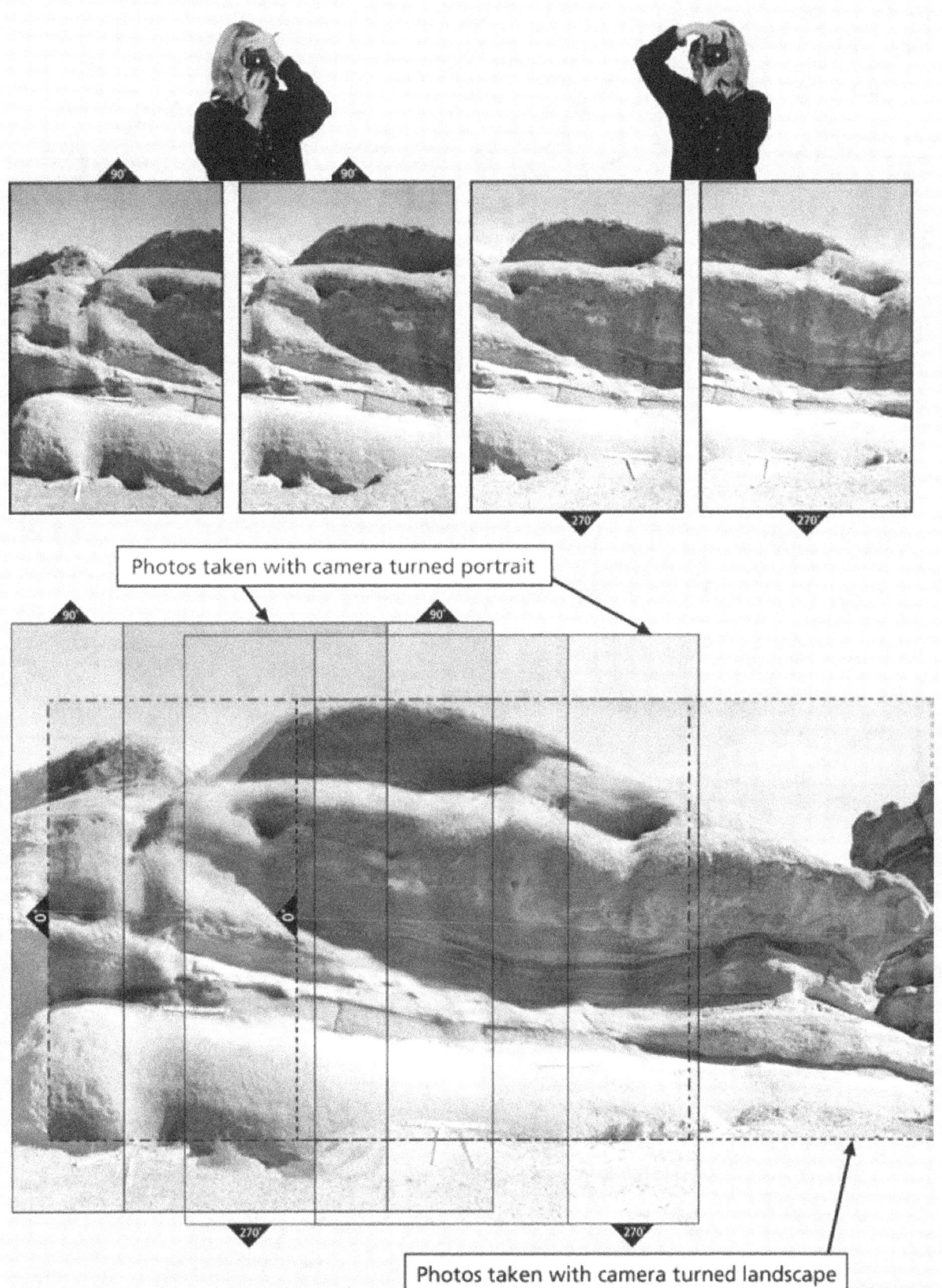

Photos taken with camera turned portrait

Photos taken with camera turned landscape

Figure D.4. The camera calibration process requires at least four additional photos. By concentrating the previously taken stereoscopic photos (landscape) and portrait-oriented photos taken at 90° and 270° over the same area, maximum benefit will be achieved in the camera calibration portion of the software.

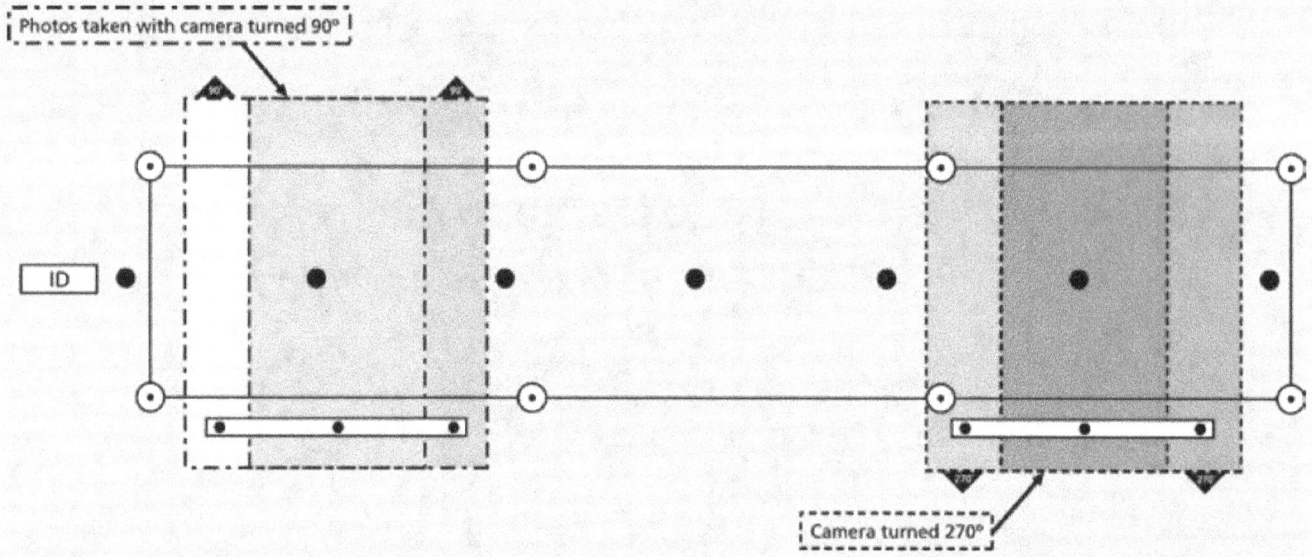

Figure D.5. To ensure project accuracy, it is necessary to take additional photographs to be used in the camera calibration process. These photos are taken at right angles, or 90° and 270°, to the sequence of stereoscopic photos and MUST use the same settings (particularly focus and focal distance). At least four photos are needed and should be stereo pairs. They may be taken at any position in the stereoscopic sequence as long as they are in common with it. At least one stereo pair must be taken with the camera turned at 90°, and then the camera should be turned 270° with another pair of photographs taken at a slightly different location.

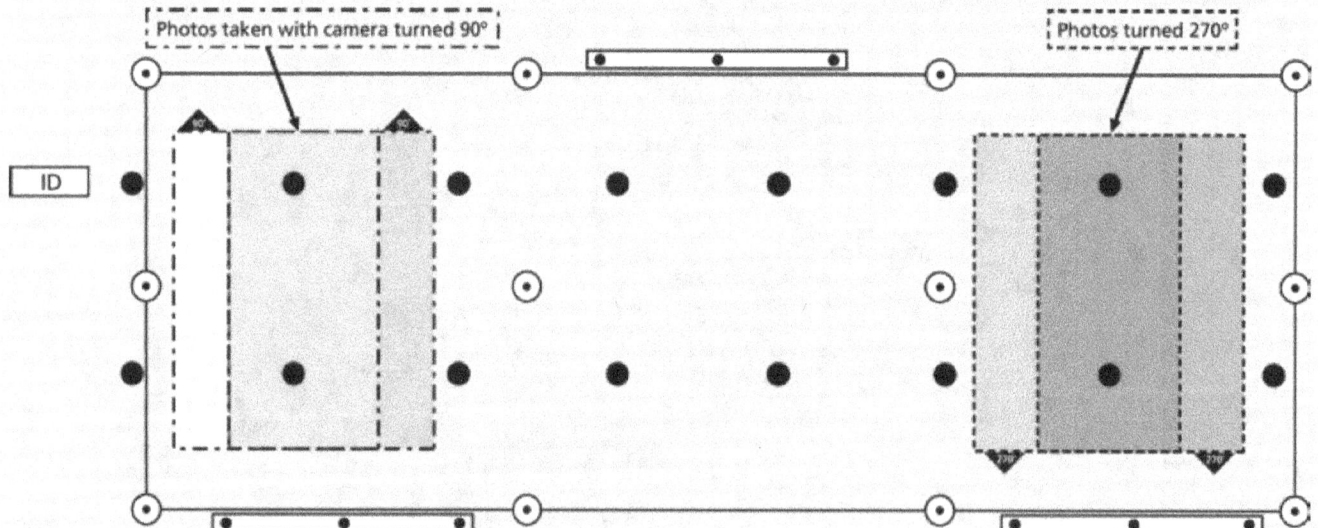

Figure D.6. Camera calibration photos for a block setup. In addition to the camera calibration, images taken in the above configuration can serve to tie the two strips together and improve accuracy (Figure D.3).

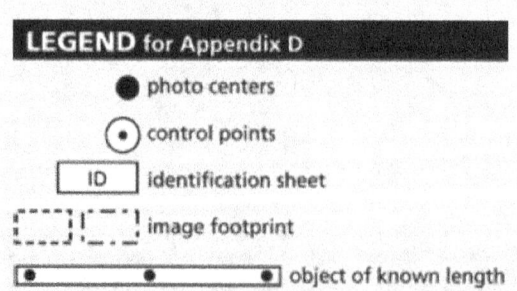

Photo Control

Another level of flexibility provided by CRP over traditional photogrammetry is in the way a subject may be controlled. Control for a user defined coordinate system can be accomplished as simply as adding an object of known dimension (meter stick, 6-inch scale, or other object) that is visible in at least two stereo models. This allows the subject to be scaled to real-world values. It is preferable to have two or more such objects, to ensure that they are visible in at least three photographs and for accuracy assessment. Experience has shown that an object of known dimension is more accurate and reliable than measuring between two points in the field. However, measuring and recording the distance between two or more points is another excellent means for confirming project accuracy.

Calibrated target sticks (CTS) may be used in addition to the object of known dimension (Figure D.7) to provide extra control, and in some instances, can help tie photos together during processing. The CTS depicted in Figure D.7 are equipped with large, black circles that are a calibrated distance apart. In addition to the calibrated circles, a series of circular bar codes (Forbes et al. 2002) can be generated within some

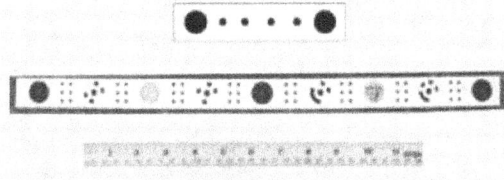

Figure D.7. Examples of calibrated target sticks (CTS) and an object of known length. The center CTS contains circular bar codes, which are used by some three-dimensional measuring and mapping software and assist with the initial image orientation process.

3DMM software. Each unique code can be recognized, correlated to the same code visible on other photographs, and marked with very little user interaction. If coded targets are not available, solid color circles of high contrast to the background (black on white) can be used by subpixel marking methods to define the center of a circle.

To tie the CRP project into a real-world coordinate system, GPS positions for known points within stereo overlap are necessary. For monitoring or other studies that require a time sequence of image capture, it is beneficial to get high-accuracy horizontal and vertical coordinates from an RTK GPS. The GPS coordinates should be taken at the monumented points; additional coordinates can also be captured for other photo recognizable features to strengthen the resolution and for accuracy checking. For projects in which location is not as critical, a resource grade GPS unit may be used and point coordinates taken at the CTS circles.

Other Considerations

Context Photos

While capturing the stereoscopic photos, it is also helpful to take an overall contextual photo (yes, you can include the horizon). It helps to remind you of how things were set up and can be used as an interesting illustration (Figure D.8). Also, make sure to get some photographs of the photogrammetric documentation in progress (Figure D.9). It is preferable to have a secondary camera (this can be a point-and-shoot), which allows photographs to be taken without disrupting the focus or settings of the primary camera.

File Management

File management is extremely important. The digital age has advanced us to where the acquisition of photographs is practically free. With the help of 3DMM softwares, photos can be used to make quantifiable measurements, transforming them from just pictures to data. Stereophotos may be used for data extraction the day they are taken, or years later. To ensure that these photos are still accessible, it is recommended that a consistent approach to file management be taken.

One strategy is to group files into directory structures that are organized by State or field office, site, date, and then by camera or lens, for example:

UTMoab/date/nik25/photos.tif

This may seem unlikely, but getting more than 10,000 close-range photographs may take a relatively short time. One of the values of the photogrammetric techniques is that photographs taken from the past (or future) can be incorporated into a project so that sites can be compared and monitored for change detection. For some projects photographed over multiple years, those digits can add up quickly.

Figure D.8. The results of merging a contextual photo with the camera locations generated in the three-dimensional measuring and mapping software are very good for displaying image relations. (Camera stations are depicted above the surface as blue rectangles and the image prints are depicted as blue and green Xs on the surface.) The image highlights locations of extreme close-range photogrammetric documentation at the Twentymile Wash Dinosaur Tracksite, Utah.

Figure D9. Work in progress at a camel trackway on BLM land near Santa Fe, New Mexico.

Preparing to take a single sequence of overlapping photographs at the Red Gulch Dinosaur Tracksite in Wyoming.

Project Workflow

The following section is a general work-flow for a small project. It is presented in outline form to serve as a guide and checklist. As the photographer becomes more familiar with the process, this list can be tailored to his or her experience and specific project requirements.

General Procedures for a Small, Close-Range Photogrammetric Project

- Evaluate subject and establish extent of the area to be photographed.
  - Assess public interactions. When working at a site visited by the public, it may be necessary to have an additional person to act as docent. This person can serve the dual function of reducing the effects of visitors on the photogrammetric process and explaining the photogrammetric work to the public.
  - Temporarily mark the area to be photographed.
  - If necessary, prepare the site by removing extraneous debris or objects that may be obscuring the terrain to be measured.
  - Sweep or clean, if hard surface. Proceed with care when documenting fragile or protected subjects!

- Determine the sun angle and best location to stand or position the tripod without casting shadows onto the subject.

- Establish final extents of project area.
  - If appropriate, place a monument with survey nails or rebar while disturbing as little of the area as possible.
  - Place CDs over each of the rebar monuments. (CDs should be painted with flat white paint). The CDs will obscure some of the sample area; however, the ground will already have been locally disturbed.

- Lay target sticks parallel to a long side, just outside the sample area.
  - Follow the photo layout (Figures D.1, D.2, D.5, and D.6)
  - Do not obscure features or control.
  - Position the target sticks along the side that the photographs will be taken from.

- Set up the tripod; attach the boom arm and add counterbalance weights to the legs, if necessary, to offset the camera if working on a slope. Set the tripod to proper height.

- Fill out the site recording sheet
  - Date
  - Site ID
  - Record next photo number.
  - Place the recording sheet clipboard on the ground outside, but near, the site.

- Set the camera to the appropriate settings (see Appendix C). Change the ISO, if necessary, for light conditions.

- Mount the camera on the tripod, adjust height, and ensure that the proper overlap is achieved.

- Set the camera to autofocus, take a picture, and inspect it for quality—focus, exposure, and other characteristics. Make adjustments as necessary.

- Once the focus is set, turn the camera to manual focus and tape the focus ring in place.

- Proceed systematically from left to right along the length of the site and take as many photos as necessary to ensure complete stereo coverage.
  - To maintain a proper 60% overlap, the camera must be moved a distance equivalent to 40% of a single photo field of view (Figure A.2).
  - Remember—the entire area must be covered by at least two overlapping photos, this will require positioning the left extant of the project in the first frame of the sequence.

- In order to create a camera calibration, take additional photos turned 90° and 270° to the previous photos:
  - At the end—turn and take a picture of the end of the site. Camera will be turned 90° and 270° to the site.
  - Go back to the start of the site and take a picture. Again, camera will be turned 90° and 270° to the site.
  - Additional 90° and 270° photos can be captured anywhere along the strip.

- When conducting several small projects in sequence, it may not be necessary to change focus or camera settings if the height remains constant. In this situation, it is helpful to have a sight recording sheet in the first image of that sequence.

  If possible, download photos and inspect for proper exposure and overlap before removing target sticks or CDs positioned on GPS control.

- Back up images (including RAW files) onto DVD or external hard drive.

Equipment Check List

___ People
  ___ Person to take photographs
  ___ Assistant to prep the site and keep track of work progress
  ___ Docent to interact with public (may be needed at visited sites) and take photos of documentation process

___ Camera and lens for CRP documentation

___ Secondary camera for backup and to document CRP process

___ Camera Accessories
  ___ Battery charger or extra batteries
  ___ Additional lenses equipped with protective bypass filters
  ___ Painter's tape or other low-adhesive tape
  ___ Spare memory cards
  ___ Remote shutter release
  ___ Lens cleaner or brush
  ___ Padded camera case

___ Laptop Computer
  ___ Card reader or appropriate cable for downloading images
  ___ Image backup—either portable hard drive or blank DVDs
  ___ Image software (preferably the software that came with the camera)
  ___ Power cord
  ___ DC adapter (if available)

___ Objects of known dimension
  ___ Commercial meter (or yard) sticks
  ___ Calibrated target sticks of varying lengths (see Figure D.8)
  ___ Removable adhesive putty may be used for temporarily securing target sticks, although even this may not be appropriate for some delicate surfaces.

___ Sturdy Tripod
  ___ Boom or extension arm
  ___ Quick release head
  ___ Extra release plates
  ___ Small screwdriver
  ___ Leg weights for camera counterbalance to keep the tripod from tipping over

___ When Establishing Location
  ___ GPS unit
  ___ Resource grade or RTK system (depending on desired product accuracy)
  ___ Survey nails or rebar
  ___ Sledge hammer, small chisel, and file
  ___ CDs spray-painted white

___ Power Accessories
  ___ Multiple-receptacle power strip
  ___ DC power inverter for car use

___ Miscellaneous Items
  ___ Measuring tape
  ___ Notebook and pencil
  ___ Pocket calculator
  ___ Small dry erase board or clipboard with identification sheet and markers
  ___ Circular disks (such as clay poker chips) to mark features or image extents
  ___ Step stool or ladder
  ___ Small tarp for shade or wind protection
  ___ Rope
  ___ Duct tape
  ___ Wisk and push brooms (when appropriate)
  ___ Tree loppers or prunners (when appropriate)
  ___ Pin flags or flagging tape
  ___ General field necessities (water, snacks, sun screen, insect repellent, hat, other items)

Setting up a GPS unit to reestablish positions for change detection at the Falcon Road Open OHV area within the Gunnison Gorge National Conservation Area near Montrose, Colorado.

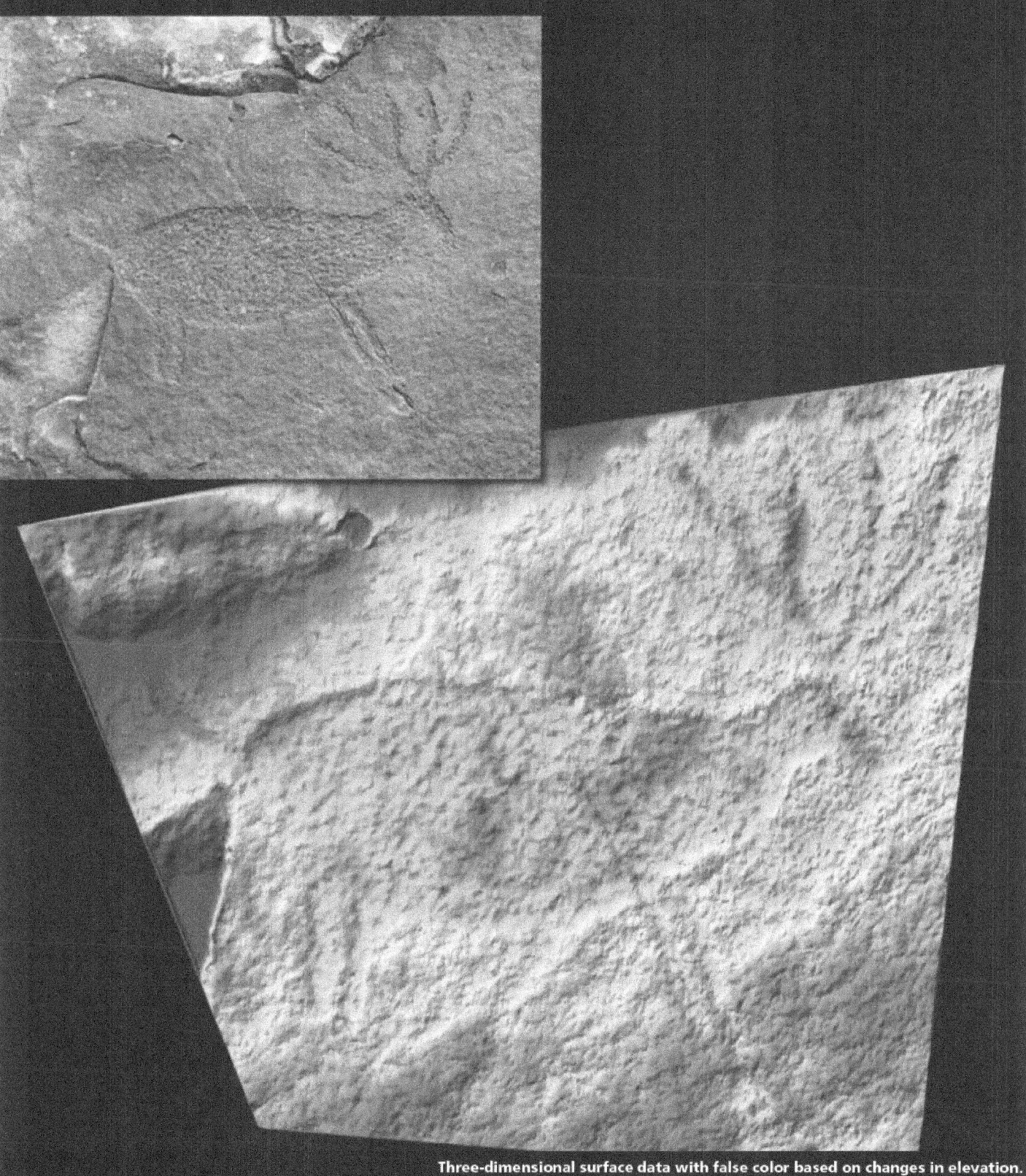

Three-dimensional surface data with false color based on changes in elevation. Image of the natural rock art surface near Newcastle, Wyoming, shown in the inset.

Oblique aerial view, taken with a large format (9 x 9 inch) aerial camera, of
Escalante Canyon in the Grand Staircase-Escalante National Monument in Utah.